The Self-Education Manual

by

Gary Dean Petersen

Self-Education Equipment & Methods

Take Charge! Teach Yourself.

Proverbs 16:16

The Self-Education Manual
by Gary Dean Petersen

Copyright © 2023 by Gary D. Petersen. *All rights reserved*

Published by Self-Education Equipment and Methods
P. O. Box 5916
Midland, TX 79704, USA

www.sem-education.com
info@sem-education.com

Publisher's Cataloging-in-Publication data

Names: Petersen, Gary Dean, author.
Title: The self-education manual / Gary Dean Petersen.
Description: Includes bibliographical references. | Midland, TX: Self-Education Equipment and Methods, L. L. C., 2024.
Identifiers: LCCN: 2021944945 | ISBN: 978-1-7366051-1-0
Subjects: LCSH Independent study. | Study skills. | Self-realization. | Goal (Psychology) | Success. |
BISAC EDUCATION / Adult & Continuing Education |
EDUCATION / Teaching / Methods & Strategies | SELF-HELP / General
Classification: LCC LB1049 .P48 2024 | DDC 371.3/.02812--dc23

Disclaimer:
As fellow learners, while we are gaining experience and expertise using the SEM Learning System, we do not claim to, as yet, be experts in the subjects we are using to teach the System.

Claims:
The SEM Learning System uses tried and true study methods. Its uniqueness and potential power derive from the orderly and synergistic grouping and sequencing of the study methods. One could say "tried and true" becomes "tried differently, and therefore, even more true."

Contents

The Impetus for *The Self-Education Manual*	7
Chapter 1: *Introduction to Learning*	11
Chapter 2: *The Work of Learning*	13
Chapter 3: *Why Before How*	14
Chapter 4: *General Principles and Instructions*	15
Chapter 5: *Tools*	19
Chapter 6: *Planning with the Decision Tree*	24
Chapter 7: *Advice on Study with Flowchart*	26
Chapter 8: *Training Scenarios*	28
Chapter 9: *Study Method Descriptions with Steps*	31
Step 1: *Relating Better to the Subject*	32
Step 2: *Identifying Learning Objects*	55
Step 3: *Making Learning Objects Memorable*	57
Step 4: *Practicing Recalling Objects*	85
Step 5: *Applying Learning Objects*	98
Chapter 10: *Begin Learning Physical Chemistry*	105
Chapter 11: *Background*	113
Epilogue	118
References	128
Metacognition and Answers	130
A Note of Encouragement from the Author	150
Illustration Credits	151
About the Author	152
A Sneak Peek of Upcoming Books: *Learning Trachtenberg Arithmetic, Learning Plane Trigonometry and True Stories*	153

NOW AVAILABLE

www.sem-education.com

In this WORKBOOK, a companion to **The Self-Education Manual**, you will find guidance for recording your work as you learn, as well as practical templates and illustrative examples. These can be used for your own learning or for teaching elementary, middle school, high school, college and adult learners.

The Impetus for
The Self-Education Manual

While working as a geologist, I got an idea to develop an invention, which subsequently inspired me to expand my science and math background. So, I enrolled in advanced physics classes to pursue an additional degree. However, two weeks into the semester, the vision in one of my eyes malfunctioned, leading to a diagnosis of a detached retina, and the treatment involved inserting a gas bubble into the eye. Since the university was situated in an area that was a thousand feet below my home, the difference in air pressure experienced while commuting posed a risk of expanding the gas bubble, potentially resulting in blindness. So, the doctor wrote a note to the university requesting my attendance be waived. Hence, I had to learn how to teach myself.

A little more than a month later, when the size of the bubble became nearly small enough that I could resume my classes, another tear occurred in my retina. Another bubble and another doctor's note intensified the need for self-learning. I ended up taking an incomplete grade in my classes.

The following semester, while I was facing the stress of the hundred-mile commute each way and the nearing exams, my remaining parent passed away. Once again, I requested and was granted more incomplete grades. Yet again, the necessity of learning how to teach myself became apparent. *The Self-Education Manual* is my attempt to share with others what I have learned about teaching myself.

Gary D. Petersen

The Self-Education Manual
by
Gary Dean Petersen

Take Charge! Teach Yourself.

Proverbs 16:16

Quick Start

When, as a teacher or as a learner, you already know of one or more learning objectives and desire to understand how people could achieve them, the following instructions can be helpful in accelerating your progress towards your goal.

1) Scan through the initial chapters to gain a preliminary understanding of all of the methods presented (they should all be somewhat familiar to you).

2) When selecting study methods to apply for a learning objective, start at Point Number Seven on the Decision Tree found on Page 21 to make an informed choice.

Chapter 1
Introduction to Learning

This *Self-Education Manual* introduces a revolutionary idea as it enables effective learning by presenting logically organized, proven study methods with new insights. Unlike typical "teaching methods," these methods are presented from the learner's perspective and empower individuals to teach themselves. Teachers could also utilize this *Manual* to guide their students in taking an active role in their learning. Before this idea, scientifically proven study methods were often obscured by jargon and buried deep in literature. Learners, teachers and parents may have been unaware of many of these methods. This *Manual* addresses the need for certain study methods for specific purposes, and often, a learning objective requires more than one method, either in combination for learning or as an additional tool for recall. This *Self-Education Manual* also attempts to resolve the challenges of choosing a study method while grappling with confusion, feeling overwhelmed, or memorization issues.

This *Manual* aims to acquaint you with sixteen effective study methods to teach yourself while guiding you on how to facilitate students or children to teach themselves. Experiments have shown that these study methods can even help people who have experienced traumatic brain injury, those who have been diagnosed with Alzheimer's disease, and even children as young as two years old. An exhaustive analysis of scientific studies on ten educational study methods (Dunlosky et al., 2013) found two of the study methods to be highly effective.

Building upon these findings, this *Manual* focuses on these two methods, linking them together and aligning all sixteen (including the ten from Dunlosky et al. and six additional ones) of the *Manual's* study methods with the idea of preparing learning objects to utilize the two proven methods. The methods are effective for both young and old people and involve practicing the recall of facts, concepts, or skills, along with strategic timing of these recall efforts.

You can be in control and succeed.

By using this *Manual*, you can gain the ability to gather and refine the learning objectives until they are memorized. After studying them and applying them in scenarios for practice, you can check your recall to prove your mastery of the desired information.

In this *Manual*, you will find summarized results from numerous reviews of studies on the effectiveness of various study methods (Dunlosky et al., 2013) along with some logical reasoning. This *Manual* has combined the less effective, yet useful, study methods to enhance their efficacy.

This *Manual* begins by introducing some general principles and instructions, followed by descriptions of study methods and examples from various subjects, where appropriate. Some examples address the needs and interests of primary-school learners, while others are for middle-school to adult learners. You will be shown how to go through the process of selecting and using one or more study methods to prepare learning objects for memorization. A Study Methods Chart, Decision Tree, and Flowchart have been provided as tools to guide the learning process.

Further, this *Manual* presents a detailed Background section comprising some of the research results for the various study methods. This section can help you understand which study methods are optimal for different types of learners and different types of information.

Please note that readers who are not confident in calculus or physics should not feel intimidated by these subjects. The calculus section merely describes how to remember an equation, not how to use it. Additionally, the Epilogue offers some advice and pictures that will be beneficial, even if the flashcards in that section may seem excessively mathematical.

It's Elementary   1

To commit this *Manual* to memory in a useful way, the "mind palace" method could be utilized as described in a conversation below from a Sherlock Holmes movie.

Dr. John Watson [about Sherlock's "mind palace"]: It's a memory technique, a sort of mental map. You plot a... a map with a location—it doesn't have to be a real place—and then you deposit memories there. Theoretically, you can never forget anything. All you have to do is find your way back to it.

Dr. Stapleton: So this imaginary location could be anything—a house, a street...?

Dr. John Watson: Yeah.

Dr. Stapleton: It's a palace. He said it was a palace.

Dr. John Watson: Yeah, well, he would, wouldn't he?

Chapter 2
The Work of Learning

When studying a subject or a textbook, where should you begin? How does one "study"? The following list outlines three phases of effective study: Phase I is preparation, Phase II is memorization and Phase III is application. To achieve the best results, all three phases should be given attention in this order. When approaching new material, the learner would do well to schedule time for each phase of the study. To provide a sense of familiarity, the study methods have been listed here; you may also check whether you are already familiar with some of them.

Please note that the sixteen study methods presented in this *Manual* may not be the only or the best ones. However, they are sufficient and highly effective in enabling readers to accomplish the work of these three phases of study.

Phase I Preparation

Phase I comprises thirteen of the sixteen study methods. It includes steps one through three, which we will discuss later. These steps entail relating better to the subject, identifying the learning objects and employing techniques to make those learning objects memorable. Step One comprises study methods such as Pre-Writing, Different Viewpoint, Interleaved Practice, Dividing Big Problems and Beachhead Strategy. Step Two involves Summarizing, Re-reading and Highlighting or Underlining. Further, Step Three comprises Why Question, Self-explanation, Keyword or Mnemonic, Mental Imagery and Simple as Pie.

Phase II Memorization

Phase II focuses on two of the sixteen study methods and is referred to later as Step Four. In this phase, we practice recalling objects. The study methods for Step Four are Practice Testing and Delayed Testing.

Phase III Application

Phase III introduces the sixteenth and final study method. Referred to later as Step Five, this phase revolves around applying learning objects. The study method for Step Five is a Learner-Generated Scenario.

Chapter 3
Why Before How

Everyone is unique. You are free to become the best version of yourself. You can choose to learn whatever captures your interest. While traditional school may be helpful, you can also choose to explore subjects that intrigue you. In this way, you can grow and develop into the person you aspire to be.

At the same time, these study methods can make it easier for you or your protégés to achieve great grades in school. While graduating and earning degrees can open doors in certain career fields, achieving such accomplishments also gives the learner satisfaction akin to winning a game. Further, achieving such milestones can also boost your confidence to conquer your goals. Education not only expands your knowledge, which could enhance your social life by providing new topics for conversations, but also gives you the ability to apply the desired new facts, concepts and skills from memory.

The methods you are about to learn may hold lasting value as you continue learning more subjects. The flashcards you create will help retain your learning for use later in life, whenever you may wish to refresh your knowledge. You should never feel that you have been out of school for too long to try learning something new. Simply save the flashcards and use them to sharpen your recall of knowledge and skills. As the diverse examples in this *Manual* will demonstrate, these methods can be applied to a wide variety of subjects, be it poker, chemistry, social studies, calculus, or any other subjects of interest.

With this *Manual*, you can learn how to learn. Since scientific studies have proved the efficacy of various study methods, you need not spend time guessing what may work or trying to invent your own. Further, scientists' insights on why certain study methods work have helped in making important improvements to some of the methods in this *Manual*. With practical examples on several subjects, this *Manual* will show you how to apply the study methods to effectively learn facts, concepts and skills.

It's Elementary   2

Developing a mind palace and practicing how to use it will facilitate real-time thinking to plan one's study time. In the *Manual*, we shall visualize a "learning vehicle" to travel through knowledge.

Chapter 4
General Principles and Instructions

A key to effective studying is actively engaging the brain in thinking about a fact, principle, or skill to be learned. Study methods that use more mental and physical learning activities are more effective than those that fail to keep the mind active. Consequently, using several learning methods would result in more mental activity, which could be more effective than using only one method. Using several methods to improve the learning of a specific fact or skill is similar to using multiple musical instruments to improve the sound of a musical piece. To streamline study sessions, after using any study method, inscribe the resulting learning objects on flashcards even if the scientific literature describing the method does not call for it. In this way, all the study sessions can utilize flashcards for review and practice.

Taking the mental effort to write one's own flashcards helps more for learning than does the buying of already-made flashcards. Writing flashcards is brain-activating and allows the flexibility of using the various study methods to form the flashcards. Flashcards are made by using index cards.

Advantages accrue if you can tell one side of a card from the other. For example, the blank side would contain a word, phrase, or similar stimulus to trigger the brain to recall the answer. Then, the learner would write this answer on the lined side to check whether what they recalled was right. In the flashcard examples appearing in this *Manual*, the top card represents the clue side, and the bottom card displays the corresponding answer.

 **It's Elementary   3**

Our imaginary learning vehicle has five general localities representing the five steps of the learning process, arranged in counter-clockwise chronological order. Each step can contain a study method in order.
 To symbolize the concept for Step One, imagine a curtain in front of the driver's view. Through the curtain, visualize a picture resembling a family tree on a stand. However, rename it as the "relative tree" to remind you of the word "relate." The stand similiar to one used to support a Christmas tree under the relative tree will remind you of the word "understand." Thus, the summary concept of Step One is "relate and understand."

Learning German:
First Example →

Animal

Tier

Skunk

← **Learning German:**
Second Example

Stinktier

The methods in this *Manual* can be utilized to learn relatively complex subjects. However, to study simpler, ready-to-learn items, such as foreign language vocabulary words, multiplication table facts, and rote memory items for preschoolers, one could use pre-made flashcards to save time. The commercial availability of some of these products is ubiquitous.

To use this *Manual*, a few supplies are required that are not included with the purchase. These supplies include 8½" x 11" spiral notebooks, 3" x 5" index cards, pencils and rubber bands for grouping flashcards. Each subject or text being studied should have its spiral notebook. You may also want to maintain a separate notebook for miscellaneous subjects, where you can occasionally develop flashcards for stray facts that you discover and desire to remember.

For several reasons, you will do well to start with a notebook and several index cards. Each fact, concept, or skill that is ready to be memorized can be made into flashcards. A major purpose of the notebook is to aid you in preparing the information to make flashcards for review and practice. In the notebook, you can record the date, your notes, the study method used and the scenarios and problems you solve. These scenarios and problems allow you to apply or use the learning object, thus acting as a memory-enhancing mental activity. Further, journaling can help in solving problems (Young, 2008). Including the date on flashcards can be helpful if you ever need to refer to where you recorded it in your notebook. Furthermore, referring to your notebook will help you remember where you left off in the previous study session.

Flashcards can be used for review and practice. Depending on your learning objectives, you may require several flashcards due to the use of several different study methods. Employing several study methods can help you develop multiple ways to recall a fact, concept, or skill. In some cases, it may be beneficial to mention the name of the study method you used on the front of the flashcard. Doing so will help you anticipate which type of answer is expected so that your response will more likely match the flip side when checking your recall. For example, **Chemistry, pouring order: (TS-13)** is prepared twice: once using mental imagery, and again using an analogy.

With some creativity and thought, you can personalize your study efforts. Some of the flashcards you design will likely only work well for you due to your unique thinking pattern and life experiences. The examples in this *Manual* have been chosen to work have been tailored to work well for the author since they have been created based on his unique thinking pattern and life experiences; hence, you may need to refine them to make them more suitable for your needs. A slightly quirky or imaginative approach can make the learning experience memorable and help in binding the learning object to memory for later recall. The result may seem ridiculous, but, if it works for you, that is what truly matters.

Soon you will find yourself visualizing the flashcards in your memory, so practice testing can be done mentally without the actual flashcards in hand. You may even find that mental images or other memory aids you have used are no longer necessary for recall. These images and aids will serve as a backup plan or a confirmation in your mind to ensure that your recall is accurate. At this point, your self-administered scaffolding has become a success (scaffolding, an educational term borrowed from the construction industry, refers to temporary support tools tailored to individual students who are not yet ready to independently use a new skill). The flashcards should, however, be kept in storage in case they are needed for future review, particularly if recall starts to become difficult due to lack of practice.

Concentration help: The author has discovered two methods to enhance concentration skills. One method entails marking a piece of paper whenever your mind wanders during study sessions. The other involves wearing a rubber band on your wrist. Then, whenever your mind wanders, lightly snap your wrist. In a few days or weeks, your concentration should reach a satisfactory level, whereupon the training will be complete.

It's Elementary   4

To visualize the concept for Step Two, image a curtain at the driver's side view that reveals the rear view mirror. Since drivers use this mirror to identify objects, it serves as a reminder for the summary concept of Step Two, "identify learning objects."

For Step Three, envision a curtain covering the side view from the left rear seat. The curtain displays someone making a photo album or scrapbook of memorabilia. The "making memorabilia" should remind you of "making memorable," which is the summary concept.

For the Step Four summary concept, imagine a curtain covering the side view from the right rear seat. On the curtain is a sticky note displaying a brain to remind you of the word "recall."

The Step Five curtain covers the side view from the right front seat. It shows a paint can and a paint brush to remind you of the summary concept "apply."

Chapter 5
Tools

This chapter introduces various tools that can be used to select the appropriate study methods. First, there is the Study Methods Chart, followed by the Decision Tree for choosing a study method, which helps in planning study sessions, and finally, the Flowchart for selecting a study method, which offers a more detailed guide and is useful for implementing the plan effectively.

These tools will prove useful, especially when initially using this *Manual*. Printed versions of these tools should be used while reading this *Manual* for efficient referencing without flipping through the pages. However, whenever the use of a study method produces a new learning object, the beginning of both the Decision Tree and the Flowchart may have to be revisited to choose from among all sixteen study methods.

Step Five of the Study Methods Chart, which involves applying the learning object, is important enough to be frequently included in the planning even if it is not immediately followed. This is similar to adhering to a guideline that says to eat healthy foods, even if you sometimes opt for what tastes good instead.

The planning scenarios in the chapter titled "Study Method Descriptions with Steps" have been set apart to avoid breaking the flow of the narrative. Braces and brackets have been used for the Decision Tree and the Flowchart, respectively, to identify the tool used in the decision-making process for selecting study methods.

It's Elementary   5

Continuing with the construction of the "learning vehicle" of the mind palace to remember the study methods, for Step One, imagine sitting in the driver's seat and looking forward, past the curtain, to see a pen as a hood ornament. The pen will help you recall the study method of <u>Pre-Writing</u>.

Next, visualize yourself turning the steering wheel. The shift in view will remind you of the study method of <u>Different Viewpoint</u>.

Now, look at the gear shift, which allows you to distinguish between and choose from among the various gears. It will remind you of the study method of <u>Interleaved Practice</u>.

Then, observe the console dividing the middle of the front seat. This division should remind you of the study method of <u>Divide Big Problems</u>.

Finally, the glove compartment contains a sand dollar to remind you of the study method of <u>Beachhead Strategy</u>.

The Study Methods Chart:

Study Methods Chart

Step	Method	Description	When or How
Step 1. Relating Better to the Subject	Pre-Writing	Write about learning subject	Difficulty relating to subject
	Different Viewpoint	Get another opinion	Let someone else explain
	Interleaved Practice	Compare and contrast	Objects seem too much alike
	Divide Big Problems	Divide and conquer	Object seems too large
	Beachhead Strategy	Find a familiar start point	Feel overwhelmed
Step 2. Identifying Learning Objects	Summarizing	Write only what is important	Boil it down
	Re-reading	Search for more	Might have missed something
	Highlighting or Underlining	Identify what is important	Choose learning object
Step 3. Making Learning Objects Memorable	Why Question	Make a why question	Ask and answer why
	Self-explanation	Explain some thing or step	Think through
	Keyword or Mnemonic	Make a symbol	Develop a reminder
	Mental Imagery	Imagine a scene	Make a mind picture
	Simple as Pie	Make an analogy	Object can be modeled
Step 4. Practicing Recalling Objects	Practice Testing	Sort flashcards	Separate cards to study more
	Delayed Testing	Wait for memory to form	Delay flashcards hours or days
Step 5. Applying Learning Objects	Learner-Generated Scenario	Invent and do ways to apply	Try scenarios or problems

Decision Tree for Choosing the Study Method

1. Are you confused?

    Yes → Proceed to #2

    No → Skip to #6

2. Are you facing difficulty relating to the subject, or do you need someone to explain it?

    Yes → Use Pre-Writing and Different Viewpoint, then proceed to #3

    No → Skip to #4

3. Are you still confused?

    Yes → Proceed to #4

    No → Skip to #6

4. Are the learning objects too similar?

    Yes → Use Interleaved Practice, then skip to #7

    No → Are the learning objects too large?

        Yes → Use Divide Big Problems, then skip to #6

        No → Proceed to #5

5. Are you feeling overwhelmed?

    Yes → Use Beachhead Strategy, then return to #1

    No → Proceed to #6

6. Have you identified the learning object?

    Yes → Proceed to #7

    No → Choose one or more of the following, then proceed to #7

        Summarizing, Re-reading, Highlighting or Underlining

7. Is the learning object ready for memorization?

    Yes → Use Practice Testing and Delayed Testing, then proceed to #8

    No → Choose one or more of the following, then repeat #7

        Why Question, Self-explanation, Keyword or Mnemonic,

        Mental Imagery, Simple as Pie

8. Learner-Generated Scenario, then return to #7, or take a break

Flowchart for Selecting a Study Method

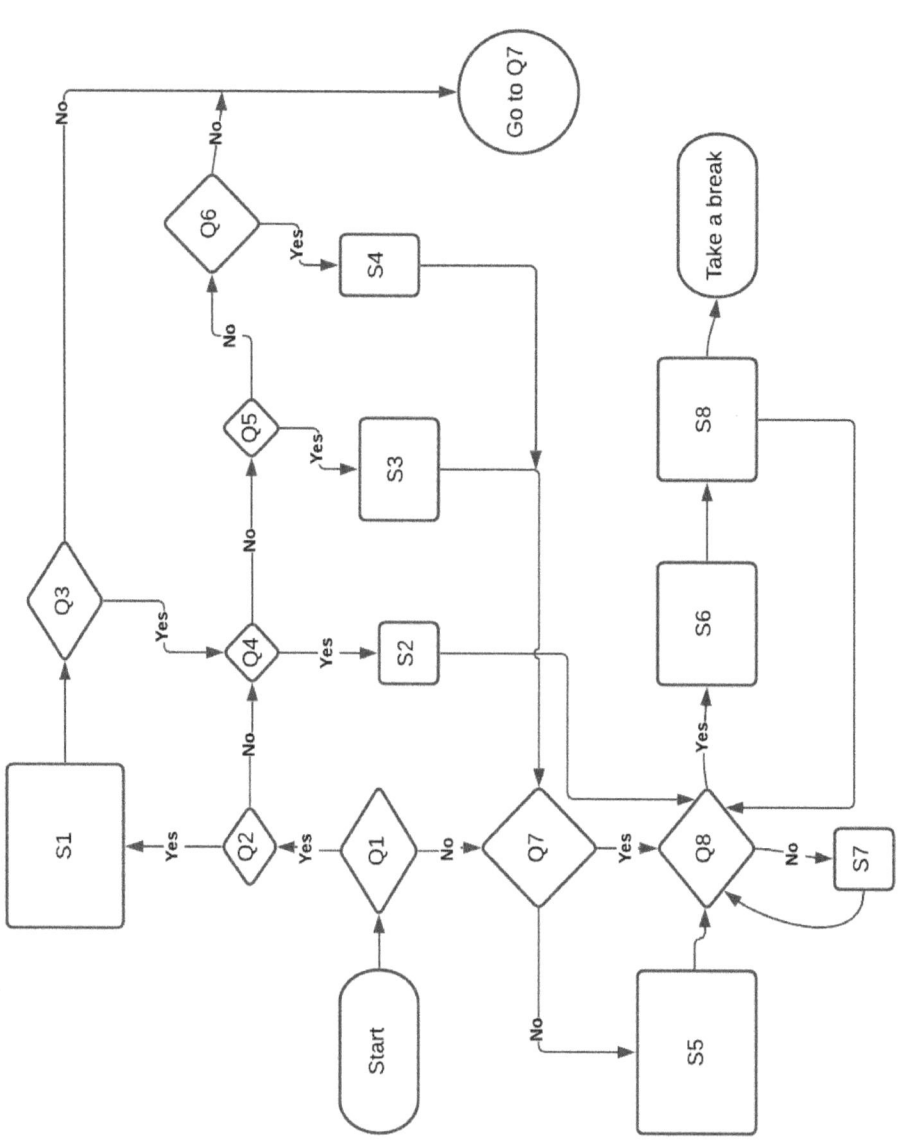

Questions and Statements for the Flowchart:

Questions:
- Q1: Are you confused?
- Q2: Are you facing difficulty relating to the subject or do you need someone to explain?
- Q3: Are you still confused?
- Q4: Are the learning objects too similar?
- Q5: Are the learning objects too large?
- Q6: Do you feel overwhelmed?
- Q7: Have you identified the learning object?
- Q8: Is the learning object ready for memorization?

Statements:
- S1: Pre-Writing and Different Viewpoint
- S2: Interleaved Practice
- S3: Divide Big Problems
- S4: Beachhead Strategy
- S5: Choose one or more of the following: Summarizing, Re-reading, Highlighting or Underlining
- S6: Practice Testing and Delayed Testing
- S7: Choose one or more of the following: Why Question, Self-explanation, Keyword or Mnemonic, Mental Imagery and Simple as Pie
- S8: Learner-Generated Scenario

It's Elementary   6

To include study methods of Step Two into the "learning vehicle" of the mind palace, imagine sitting in the driver's seat and looking to your left. Look at the top or high part of the side window and the low or under part which will remind you of <u>Highlighting or Underscoring</u>.

On the window, visualize the math problem "2 + 2 = 4." This sum will remind you of <u>Summarizing</u>.

Look at the door handle used to reopen the door. This reopening will remind you of <u>Reading and Re-reading</u>.

To remember the study methods of Step Three, visualize yourself sitting in the left rear seat and looking to your left past the curtain. At the top of the window, visualize a question mark to remind you of the <u>Why Question</u>.

At the left edge of the window, imagine an exclamation point to remind you of <u>Self-explanation</u>.

Resting on the bottom edge of the window, visualize a key to remind you of a <u>Keyword or Mnemonic</u>.

Attached to the door handle, imagine a brain and an eye to remind you of <u>Mental Image</u>.

On the right edge of the window, visualize either the symbol for pi (π), or a small circular pie with a missing piece to remind you of <u>Simple as Pie</u>.

Chapter 6
Planning with the Decision Tree

The chapter titled "The Work of Learning" introduced three phases of learning, the first of which was preparation. In this phase, thirteen of the sixteen study methods are employed to prepare learning objects for the phases of memorization and application. Using the Decision Tree is a quick and easy way to plan which study methods to use. After this simplified planning, one can then employ the more detailed Flowchart to work the plan.

In the current chapter, we assume the role of a learner in several learning situations. The first learning situation involves learning how we know the size of the Sun and how far from Earth it is. Use of the Decision Tree is denoted by enclosure with braces. {(1) Yes, (2) Yes, Pre-Writing and Different Viewpoint, (3) No, (6) Yes, (7) No, Self-explanation, Keyword or Mnemonic and Mental Imagery, (7) Yes, Practice Testing and Delayed Testing, (8) Choose, to investigate as a Learner-Generated Scenario, how we know the size of Mars and how far it is from Earth.} Stripping the numbers and Yes/No decisions from this effort yields a planned list of study methods as follows.

> Plan to learn how we know the size of the Sun and its distance from Earth:
> * Pre-Writing and Different Viewpoint
> * Self-explanation, Keyword or Mnemonics and
>   Mental Imagery
> * Practice Testing and Delayed Testing
> * Learner-Generated Scenario: Learn how we know
>   the size of Mars and its distance from Earth.

Again, for more detail, the Flowchart may be employed for the actual learning attempt, which might differ from the plan as unforeseen information comes to light. The next learning situation involves reviewing and learning the Law of Cosines and its intended uses. The plan above for learning the quadratic equation might be used also for learning of the Law of Cosines. The second part of our objective in this scenario is to learn the intended uses of the Law of Cosines. {(1) Yes, (2) Yes, Pre-Writing and Different Viewpoint, (3) No, (6) Yes, (7) No, Self-explanation, Keyword or Mnemonic and Mental Imagery, (7) Yes, Practice Testing and Delayed Testing, (8) Learner-Generated Scenario, Take a break.} Stripping the numbers and Yes/No decisions from this effort yields a planned list of study methods.

Plan to learn the uses of the Law of Cosines:
- * Pre-Writing and Different Viewpoint
- * Self-Explanation, Keyword or Mnemonics and Mental Imagery
- * Practice Testing and Delayed Testing
- * Learner-Generated Scenario

Next, as before, we employ the Flowchart for performing the actual learning attempt. Again, the actual methods chosen might differ from the plan due to the emergence of unforeseen information.

It's Elementary   7

To include the study methods of Step Four into the "learning vehicle" of the mind palace, imagine sitting in the rear passenger side seat and looking to the right. Visualize a "T" shape (perhaps made of boards) on the window. On the vertical part of the T, imagine the word "Practice", and on the horizontal part of the T, the word "Delayed". The T itself will remind you of the word "Testing". Thus, you will be able to recall the two study methods as <u>Practice Testing</u> and <u>Delayed Testing</u>.

For the study method of Step Five, imagine yourself sitting in the front seat on the passenger side and looking right. On the window, imagine an image (using a lot of imagination) of a student cranking a hand-powered generator to produce a sombrero. This will remind you of the name of the final study method, called <u>Learner-Generated Scenario</u>.

Chapter 7
Advice on Study with Flowchart

We have just discussed study planning using the Decision Tree. The Decision Tree will help quickly and easily select study methods to create a study plan. The Flowchart employs logic which is similar to that used by the Decision Tree, but it also visually represents some of the details of the reasoning in the branches of the decision-making process. In so doing, the advantage of using the Flowchart is to allow the learner to see the thinking process in order to stimulate ideas. To see an example of this, after you have read Chapter 9, see the end of the Epilogue for a discussion of using the Beachhead Strategy to study physical chemistry. The initial planning can be done without showing this amount of detail.

As with any modeling effort, the model is, alas, not perfect. A perfect model would bear the risk of being impractically long and complicated to account for all the possibilities. This chapter reveals some of the adjustments needed to enable this imperfect model to work in a wide range of scenarios.

One such case is when using the study method called Different Viewpoint, and it becomes evident that some essential knowledge is missing. At this point, stop the learning attempt and take a detour. First, learn the prerequisite knowledge to proceed with a modicum of potential for success. Without the necessary prerequisite knowledge, the learning process becomes similar to a puzzle with missing pieces, making completion impossible.

Another adjustment is sometimes needed when, in the course of using the study method called Learner-Generated Scenario, one generates a new learning object. If the new learning object is ready to memorize or ready to be made memorable, then the Flowchart works as it is. However, if the new object is not ready to proceed in either of those ways, then, to learn it requires starting over at the beginning of the Decision Tree.

When the learner is at S6, attempting to use the study methods called Practice Testing and Delayed Testing, and becomes aware of a wish to develop yet another way to remember a particular learning object, go on to S8: Learner-Generated Scenario and follow the arrow back to Q8 and say No. This brings the learner back to S7, to make different choices of ways to make the learning object memorable before proceeding back to S6, equipped with the fruits of the new set of study method choices.

When the learning objective is overwhelming and must be learned one piece at a time, each piece means starting over with the Decision Tree; however, the same plan can likely be reused for each piece. The same can be said of the actual learning attempt with the Flowchart.

Chapter 8
Training Scenarios

After you have acquired some experience with the various study methods, you may find it second nature to choose and apply them. Until that day arrives, you should utilize the tools shown in Chapter 5 to guide your choices and learning activities.

To orient the reader, this chapter explains training scenarios that accompany selected examples, many found presented in the chapter titled "Study Method Descriptions with Steps." These scenarios, mostly in the chapter "Metacognition and Answers," are set apart from the flowing narrative to minimize disruption of readability for those who prefer reading first and training later.

Each scenario has two parts. To train yourself in the correct use of the tools, you could start by finding interesting examples in that chapter and, while referring to the Study Methods Chart and the Decision Tree, try to develop your own planned lists of study methods to go with the examples. Then, compare your lists with the first part of the training scenarios, which are located in the chapter "Metacognition and Answers." Both the training scenarios and their answers have matching identifying numbers, such as TS-1 and TS-2.

For practice, each example should be treated as if one would want to remember it. That way, one can plan how to remember the learning object, just for the practice, rather than just cavalierly skipping subjects in which you may not actually be interested.

Then, as you follow the plan, use the Flowchart and record a list of the study methods you use. Again, you could compare your approach—this time with the second part of the training scenarios—to check against one exemplary correct way to work the study plan. For convenience, use separate physical copies of each of the three tools. Otherwise, you may have to frequently turn the pages to locate and refer to the tools.

To become proficient with using the Learning Tool Kit, repeat this procedure of planning, implementing plans and checking your work several times. When ready, try learning something outside this *Manual*. And if desired, you can also become equipped to design lessons for your protégés, such as children, students, or care recipients. When they are ready, you can guide them in using these methods to acquire new learning objects beyond those found in this *Manual*.

For use by learners and teachers of learners

Suggested Grading Rubric

Correct planning and use of <u>study methods</u>: **70 points**
<u>Flashcards</u>* from rote only to enhanced memory clues: **5 to 20 points**
Second way to remember: **5 points**
Learner-Generated Scenario**: **5 points**
Total: **100 max points**

---

*Flashcard grading detail
Examples from learning German:
1) Hint: Animal; Answer: Tier - **Points: 5**

2) Hint: Skunk; Answer: Stink is a clue, so, Stinktier - **Points: 20**

3) Hint: Animal; Answer: Animal reminds of pet, which, when dead brings a tear. Tear and Tier sound alike (for a non-rote memory clue) - **Points: 20**

4) Hint: Skunk; Answer: Skunk's stink reminds of onion, which brings a tear. So, stink-tear, which reminds of "Stinktier" - **Points: 20**

**Learner-Generated Scenario detail
    Example: Use vocabulary words in a sentence. Stinktier is a Tier. Or, all in German: Stinktier ist ein Tier. (In English: Skunk is an animal.)

An exercise involving a practical simulation follows. This exercise gives pointers through considering a simulated real-life scenario. Say you decide to try to learn five new things by noon. Where should you start? See below.

Learn Five Things by Noon
<u>Define learn.</u> Make a learning plan with the Decision Tree, at a minimum. Also, start implementing the plan with the Flowchart. Learning is a process which takes time. Processes can entail the phases of starting, finishing and following-through. Studying is ongoing to maintain retention of learning over time.

Set out equipment and materials. Here is a good list.
   1) Source, such as a textbook
   2) Learning Tool Kit
   3) Spiral notebook designated to go with this source
   4) Pencil or pen
   5) Eraser
   6) Some unused index cards
   7) A couple of rubber bands
   8) Scratch paper
   9) *The Self-Education Manual*

Form a basic starting study plan using the Decision Tree. For this exercise, assume you have not yet looked at the source. You may use this plan as a generic one. The result is below.

{(1) Yes, (2) Yes, Pre-Writing and Different Viewpoint, (3) Yes, (4) No, too large, No, (5) No, (6) No, Choose one or more of the following: Summarizing, Re-reading, Highlighting or Underlining, (7) No, Choose one or more of the following: Why Question, Self-explanation, Keyword or Mnemonic, Mental Imagery, Simple as Pie, (7) Yes, Practice Testing and Delayed Testing, (8) Learner-Generated Scenario, Take a break.}

Next, purge numbers and Yes/No decisions above to yield the study plan.

* Pre-Writing and Different Viewpoint
* Choose from Summarizing, Re-reading,
    Highlighting or Underlining
* Choose from Why Question, Self-explanation,
    Keyword or Mnemonic, Mental Imagery,
    Simple as Pie
* Practice Testing and Delayed Testing
* Learner-Generated Scenario

Implement the plan using the Flowchart. Keep in mind that whenever you use a study method and it creates a new learning object, you may need to go back to the beginning of both the Decision Tree and the Flowchart so that you can choose the most effective study method from all sixteen.

Chapter 9
Study Method Descriptions with Steps

Refer to the Study Methods Chart on Page 20.

The study method descriptions in the *Manual* comprise five steps, which can be loosely compared to driving a vehicle. Step One clears your mind of confusion, as a confused mindset is unsafe for driving. Step Two is similar to consulting a map. It is required to identify the next step when a large learning object is being learned one piece at a time.

Step Three acts as the engine, where the work of making learning objects memorable is accomplished, unless the learning objects are ready to be placed on flashcards. Step Four represents the driver's education phase, where the learning objects (on flashcards) are studied and practice-tested. Lastly, Step Five is where the rubber meets the road or where the learning objects are applied and used. Note that this analogy is an example of the Simple as Pie study method of Step Three.

If you encounter something you're ready to learn (Step One using five study methods and Step Two using three study methods), then create and use flashcards (Step Four using two study methods) to help remember them and use scenarios or problems to apply them (Step Five using one study method). If the object is not ready to be learned, enhance it first by using the five study methods of Step Three.

Step 1
Relating Better to the Subject

Refer to the Study Methods Chart on Page 20.

Before learning any new material, one should first understand it. When confusion arises, here are five pertinent methods to consider. Generally, the first two methods, Pre-Writing and Different Viewpoint should be tried first [Start, Q1 – Yes, Q2 – Yes, S1] [The last two study methods of this step are similar. They are reached in the Flowchart by choosing "Yes" for Q5 or Q6. Hence, decide whether you feel more strongly about a) the learning object is too large or b) being overwhelmed. If you choose b, then choose "No" for Q5, which brings you to Q6, where you should choose "Yes" to get to S4.]

 Pre-Writing

Pre-Writing is a frequently helpful method that addresses conflicts arising from the differences between one's expectations of how the material should be presented and its actual presentation in a book or a lecture. For example, you may expect a logical, orderly presentation, only to find one that jumps around almost unpredictably.

Due to such conflicts, students may misread a text or misunderstand a professor. It is similar to when the audience is unable to understand how a trick is done because the magician has distracted them. So, if you cannot seem to relate to a subject, perhaps this method will be helpful.

To use this method, simply write about the learning object and its significance in your life. During this process, you may come up with a helpful strategy and, effectively, answer the question "Is this item worth my effort to learn?" This conflict, called cognitive dissonance (Festinger, 1957), has been shown to decrease or be eliminated through this method (Kalman et al., 2015).

It is logical to assume that this Pre-Writing method partly explains why journaling helps in problem-solving. Writing about problems can similarly reduce confusion, aiding in conflict resolution.

Several examples of the Pre-Writing study method are provided later in this chapter. For one such example, refer to Different Viewpoint, Chess.

 **Different Viewpoint**

The second method, also frequently helpful, is Different Viewpoint (Bollen et al., 2016; Petersen & Michael, 2017; White et al., 2016). In this approach, you may talk to classmates, read different books or watch YouTube videos to gain a fresh understanding. In other words, you rely on someone else to help explain the material. However, keep in mind that, sometimes, prerequisite information must be learned before comprehending the currently sought information. If so, take the time to learn the prerequisite information before proceeding.

In this *Manual*, the term "Different Viewpoint" can include any information source outside of your mind. When choosing such a source, consider your usual learning style, such as auditory, visual, or kinesthetic.

Below are examples of using the Different Viewpoint method:

Wrestling: The author of this *Manual* viewed several YouTube videos to clear up confusion regarding the use of the "whizzer," as demonstrated by the wrestling coach of Washington State University. Since the term sounds like a lively move, the author assumed that the movements in the demonstration were the whizzer; however, different demonstrations portrayed different motions. The videos posted on YouTube gradually made it clear that the whizzer is a clinch hold with which one can try different moves. Thus, the whizzer is a hold and not a move. For an example of how to form a study plan for this subject, refer to the chapter titled "Metacognition and Answers" under the heading "TS-1 Whizzer."

Chess: Imagine you want to advance from proficiency to an expert level in chess. To learn various popular moves, use the Different Viewpoint method by conducting a web search for "fool's mate," "chess traps" and "queen's gambit." While exploring the results of your research, you may notice the need to learn the numbering system for a chessboard. In this case, you could start with the Pre-Writing study method to plan the objective and how to approach it. Let us try it.

Start by writing the following: "We not only need to learn the numbering pattern but need to be familiar with it and use it. Perhaps breaking it down into quadrants will be helpful."

Based on what you remember from your online research, use the lines of a notebook to number from the "White's" perspective and draw lines to divide the board into quadrants.

For an example of how to form a study plan, see the chapter titled "Metacognition and Answers" under the heading "TS-2 Chess."

```
     a    b    c    d    e    f    g    h
 8                       |                       8
 7                       |                       7
 6                       |                       6
 5_____|_____5
 4                       |                       4
 3                       |                       3
 2                       |                       2
 1                       |                       1
     a    b    c    d    e    f    g    h
```

Notice the queens will both start in Column d.
Kings start in Column e.
Rooks start in Column a or h.
Knights start in Column b or g.
Bishops start in Column c or f.
White pawns first move to Row 3 or 4.
Black pawns first move to Row 6 or 5.

Thus, we have seven facts that can be placed on flashcards for the Practice Testing method. [Start, Q1 – Yes, Q2 – Yes, S1, Q3 – No, Q7 – Yes, Q8 – Yes, S6] As you proceed, create a mental image of the numbering system. For example:

In which column do both queens start?

d

Continue in this vein. More chess examples will be introduced later with another study method.

 Interleaved Practice

The third method for dealing with a certain kind of confusion is Interleaved Practice. This study method helps clarify the confusion caused by similar learning objects that are not easily distinguishable. The Interleaved Practice study method involves grouping flashcards with similar learning objects, allowing you to study and practice-test the similar objects together.

So, when several learning objects seem too alike, comparing and contrasting them can be helpful. This method helps the learner notice and learn minute differences between similar objects. That way, you enhance your ability to recall the correct answer, preventing confusion between different answers. This method does not always generate new flashcards but rather is a grouping strategy for the existing flashcards.

Algebra, circle: (TS-3)

Circle circumference formula

Example from Math →

$2\pi r$

Circle area formula

A Second Example from Math ←

πr^2

Later, the slight differences in these similar answers are noted and explained to prevent confusing them as examples of another study method.

 Divide Big Problems

The fourth method to reduce confusion is called "Divide Big Problems." This approach involves breaking up a large learning object into smaller problems, solving them individually, and then putting the results back together. First, solve the smaller components, as shown in the example below.

Math, multiplication: (TS-4) Learning the multiplication table can require a lot of flashcards. When a student forgets a multiplication fact, such as 8 x 6, practiced) this backup plan: go to Step One and try the Divide Big Problems study method. Using the distributive law, split the problem into smaller parts (Zimmerman, 2018). Replace the larger number (in this case, 8) with a sum of small numbers (such as 4 + 4 or 6 + 2) and then multiply them by the smaller number (in this case, 6) and finally add up the results. Stepwise, this would be presented as follows:

1. 8 x 6
2. (4 + 4) x 6
3. (4 x 6) + (4 x 6)
4. 24 + 24
5. 48

or,

1. 8 x 6
2. (6 + 2) x 6
3. (6 x 6) + (2 x 6)
4. 36 + 12
5. 48

Now, using the Self-explanation study method from Step Three, make flashcards. [Start, Q1 – Yes, Q2 – Yes, S1, Q3 – No, Q7 – Yes, Q8 – No, S7, Self-explanation, Q8 – Yes, S6]

Explain what to do when
you forget a multiplication fact.

Split one number into a sum in parentheses.
Multiply by the other number and add up the results.

When practicing with this flashcard, the student may go to Step Five and revisit other forgotten facts to ensure the concept has been correctly learned and can be applied when needed. This is an example of the Learner-Generated Scenario study method.

You forget a multiplication fact like 5 x 9.

$5 \times 9 = 5 \times (5 + 4) = 5 \times 5 + 5 \times 4 = 25 + 20 = 45$

Training Item

Math multiplication: Planning

PART 1: {(1) Yes, (2) Yes, Pre-Writing and Different Viewpoint, (3) Yes, (4) No, too large, Yes, Divide Big Problems, (6) Yes, Practice Testing and Delayed Testing, (8) Learner-Generated Scenario, Take a break}

Purge numbers and Yes/No decisions to yield a study plan.

The plan for remembering what to do when you forget a multiplication fact is as follows:
* Pre-Writing and Different Viewpoint
* Divide Big Problems
* Self-explanation
* Practice Testing and Delayed Testing
* Learner-Generated Scenario

PART 2: [Q1 Yes, Q2 Yes, S1, Pre-Writing and Different Viewpoint, Q3 Yes, Q4 No, Q5 Yes, S3, Divide Big Problems, Q7 Yes, Q8 No, S7, Self explanation, Q8 Yes, S6, Practice Testing and Delayed Testing, S8, Learner-Generated Scenario: "12 x 6," Q8 No, S7, Self-explanation, Q8 Yes, S6, Practice Testing and Delayed Testing, S8, Learner-Generated Scenario, Take a break]

Purge numbers and Yes/No decisions to obtain study methods of actual learning attempts:

* Pre-Writing and Different Viewpoint
* Divide Big Problems
* Self-explanation
* Practice Testing and Delayed Testing
* Learner-Generated Scenario
* Try the problem 12 x 6
* Self-explanation
* Practice Testing and Delayed Testing
* Learner-Generated Scenario

Note: Planned study methods and the actual learning attempt may differ for a new problem, such as 12 x 6.

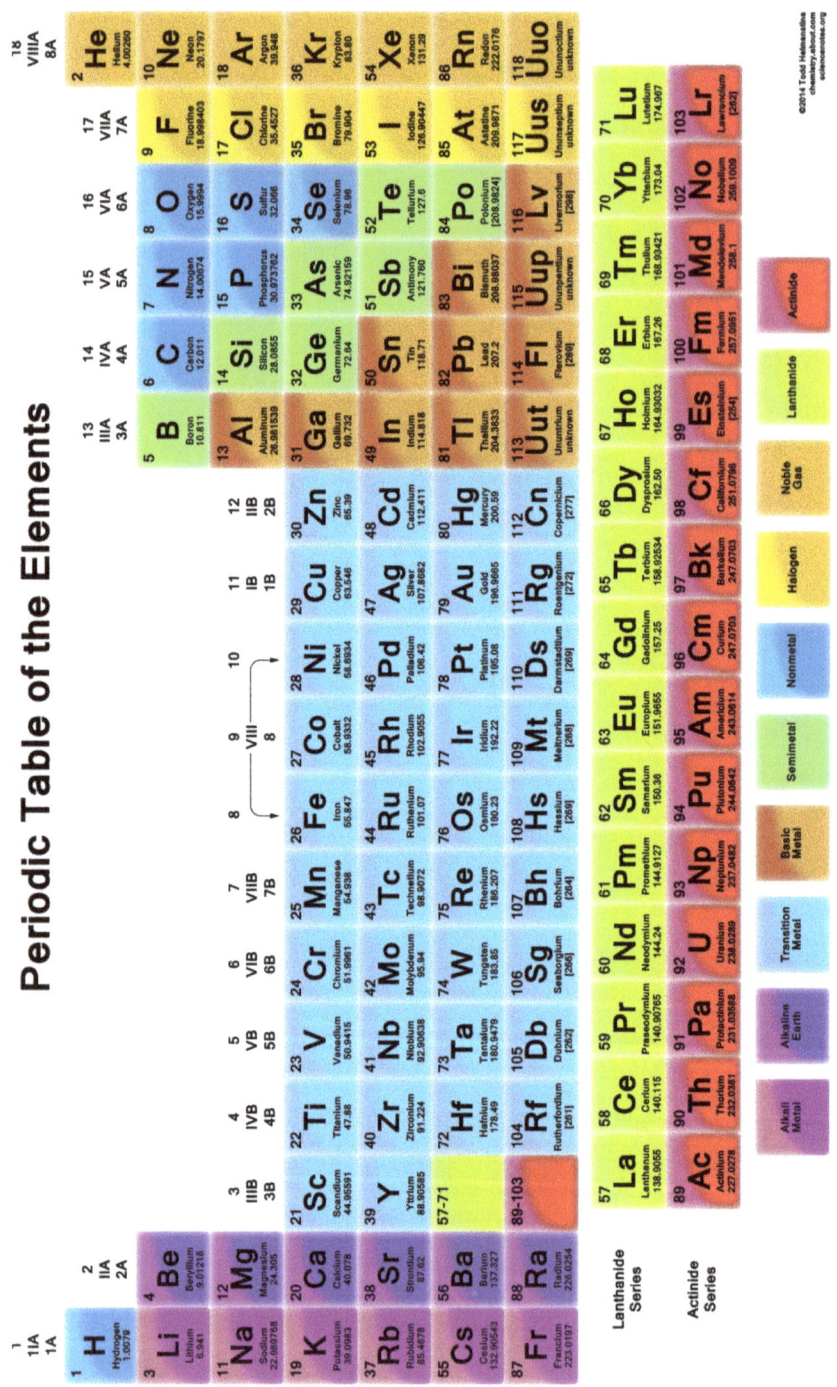

Memorizing the periodic table (Helmenstine, 2017) can be a daunting task, but in countries like Kenya and Bangladesh, which use British education materials, it is not considered so. When monetary considerations make it impossible for every student to have a textbook, the periodic table is memorized as a necessity. Could the study methods in this *Manual* help? Possibly. Rather than attempt the feat and risk repeating some previously demonstrated study methods, we shall undertake a less lofty and time- and effort-consuming enterprise.

Begin with Step One by using the Divide Big Problems study method, and identify some learning objects. First, start with five groups of seven elements. The first and last columns look like tall bookends that are seven elements high. The last column contains the noble gases, while there are also seven semimetals, seven nonmetals and seven diatomic gasses: hydrogen, nitrogen, oxygen and the first four halogens. Additionally, there are three groups of six elements: alkali metals, alkaline earth metals, and halogens. The remaining sections of the table contain the basic metals, the transition metals, the lanthanide series and the actinide series.

Several of these element groupings have been chosen as examples for other study methods, which will appear later.

 Beachhead Strategy

The fifth method is the Beachhead Strategy, named after the Allied invasion of Normandy during World War II. It may be useful while studying physics, where information is so interdependent that to learn anything, one must first learn everything else (Fogiel, 1976). The Beachhead Strategy involves choosing small, independent starting points, perhaps as extensions of previously learned math problems.

From these beachheads, one can gradually explore and conquer an enormous field of study. In physics, for instance, one could start with a trigonometry or calculus text and search for problems or index items that use physics terminology. So, when facing overwhelming learning objects, starting with a beachhead can be helpful.

Geology, timescale: (TS-5) The task of memorizing the chart of geologic periods shown on the next page (It's a Natural Universe, 2015) seems daunting because of its size. To tackle it, choose the Beachhead Strategy in Step One.

Start by choosing parts of the chart, generally by moving left to right or top to bottom. As we proceed, you may notice that other methods should also be employed to conquer the chart. While learning the material, consider starting in a different place or choosing different-sized sections of the chart to learn in one study session.

Although the task seems tedious, the author's example helped him learn the names and order of the various times and important points. If you are not ready for this level of detail, feel free to skip it for now and try again when you are ready.

Geological Time Scale (Mya = million years ago)

Eon	Era	Period		Epoch	Mya
Phanero-zoic	Cenozoic (mammals)	Quaternary		Holocene	0.01
				Pleistocene	1.8
		Tertiary	Neogene	Pliocene	5.3
				Miocene	23
			Paleogene	Oligocene	35
				Eocene	55
				Paleocene	65.5
	Mesozoic (dinosaurs)	Cretaceous (S. America, Africa)			146
		Jurassic (Alps/Himalaya)			200
		Triassic (Pangea)			251
	Paleozoic (inverte-brates)	Permian			299
		Carboniferous	Pennsylvanian		320
			Mississippian		359
		Devonian (fish)			416
		Silurian			444
		Ordovician			488
		Cambrian (Pannotia, Rodinia)			542
Pre-cambrian	Proterozoic (O2-rich atmosphere)	Ediacaran			635
					2500
	Archean (appearance of life)				3800
	Hadean				4700

(It's a Natural Universe, 2015) The geologic time scale is used without alteration.

Let us begin with the column headings—Eon, Era, Period and Epoch. As a start, we can remember them by jotting down some observations and potentially relevant thoughts from the chart.

Observations: "Eons ago" is a common phrase meaning long ago, and "Eon" appears first from the left. Following that is "Era," which is also a short word that starts with an "E." "Period" can be linked to the punctuation at the end of a sentence, and it appears at the end of the columns, except for "Epoch." There were no mammals before the epoch, which was 65.5 million years ago. To remember "epoch," think of epoxy glue and picture millions of animals stuck with epoxy glue near the age of social security.

The current eon is called the Phanerozoic Eon. To remember this, imagine a hot, ancient zoo with animals fanning themselves. This eon started 542 million years ago, so observing the animals are five slightly balding, pudgy, 42-year-old zookeepers holding a sign with "542" written on it.

There were only three eons before that, which were jointly referred to as Precambrian and started 4.7 billion years ago. To remember this, picture a high-school student holding a bill for a pre-calculus book with "4.7" written on it.

First geologic time chart column heading (from common phrase for long ago)

"Eons ago," so the left-most column heading on the geologic chart is Eon.

Second column heading of the geologic time chart, and how it is like the first

Eon	Era
Phanero-zoic	Cenozoic (mammals)

The second column heading on the geologic chart is also a short word starting with E, namely Era.

Memory keywords for the third and fourth column headings of the geologic time chart

Period	Epoch
	Holocene

Period can mean punctuation at the end of a sentence and is last, except for epoxy glue, which reminds one of Epoch.

Mental image for Epoch information

Millions of current animals stuck as with epoxy glue near the social security age

Mental image for the next eon after the oxygen-rich one

Oxygen molecules produced by an archaic plant with 3.8 written in red on the stem

Geologic time chart column headings

Eon	Era	Period		Epoch
Phanero-zoic	Cenozoic (mammals)	Quaternary		Holocene
				Pleistocene
		Tertiary	Neogene	Pliocene
				Miocene
			Paleogene	Oligocene
				Eocene

Eon, Era, Period and Epoch

Image for current Eon

Ancient zoo animals fanning themselves. Observing the animals are five slightly balding, pudgy 42-year-old zookeepers holding a sign with 542 written on it.

What is the current eon, and when did it start?	What is the group name for the oldest batch of eons, and when did they start? How many are there?

↓ ↓

The current eon is the Phanerozoic Eon, which began 542 million years ago.	The 3 Precambrian Eons are the oldest, having started 4.7 billion years ago.

Make these flashcards and use them for practice. Then, take a break before repeating the process with other sections of the chart. [Q1 – Yes, Q2 – Yes, S1, Q3 – Yes, Q4 – No, Q5 – No, Q6 – Yes, S4, Q7 – No, S5, Q8 – No, S7, Q8 – Yes, S6, S8].

After the break, repeat the process using the Beachhead Strategy. Focus on the three Precambrian Eons and the three eras of the Phanerozoic Eon for memorization. Write down observations and use them to help in remembering the information. Select reminder words and create a mental image to remember the keywords.

Observations: The three Precambrian Eons are Proterozoic (starting at 2.5 billion years ago) with an oxygen-rich atmosphere, Archean (starting at 3.8 billion years ago) with the appearance of life and Hadean with no life. The three eras are Cenozoic (same time as the epochs), Mesozoic (starting 251 million years ago) with dinosaurs and Paleozoic with invertebrates. The first eon below the current one ends with the same five letters. The atmosphere was rich in oxygen, possibly with protozoans, thus the name Proterozoic. To form a mental image of the next eon below the first, create an "O" shape with the five letters at the end of the first eon to remind you of the oxygen-rich atmosphere. Imagine that the "O" is a magnifying lens to see a protozoan shaped like a duck bill with a green 2.5 painted on it for 2.5 billion years ago.

Next, Archean sounds archaic, reminding one of the old or first life. Think of an archaic plant with 3.8 written in red on the stem. Finally, Hadean sounds like Hades, which is a place unfit for life, so remember that there was no life.

The three eras cover the same time as the current eon and share the same last five letters. The first few letters are Cen, Mes and Pale. Visualize a centurion (Roman soldier) who is mesmerized by 25 one-dollar coins and has a pale face. He is standing next to the current era because they cover the same years.

Now, we can design flashcards for these observations.

Mental image of next eon below the first, current one

The five letters at the end of the first eon are arranged to make an O shape to remind you of the oxygen-rich atmosphere. The O is a magnifying lens looking at a protozoan shaped like a duck bill with a green 2.5 painted on it for 2.5 billion years ago.

Using a mental image, name the next eon below the current one and tell something about it and when it started.

The Proterozoic Eon started 2.5 billion years ago and had an oxygen-rich atmosphere.

Using a mental image, when did epochs start and what do we know of them?

Epochs started 65.5 million years ago, when mammals appeared.

The platypus is an example of a monotreme, an early branching of the mammalian family tree.

Using a mental image for the second Precambrian Eon, name it and tell when it started and something about it.

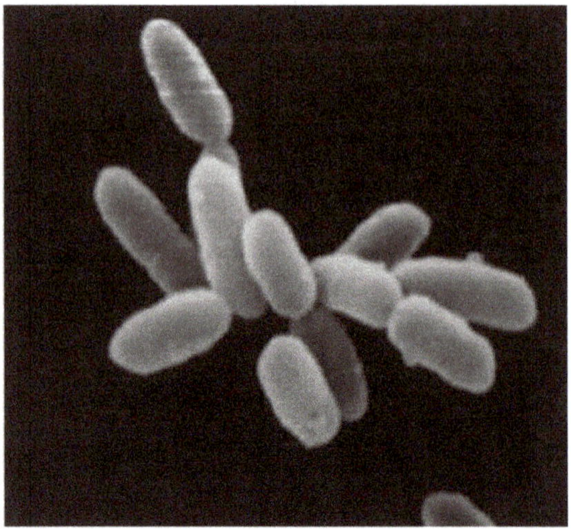

The Archean Eon started 3.8 billion years ago and showed the first signs of life.

Archaea microbes

From a mental image for the oldest eon, name it.

Hadean = Lifeless

The oldest eon preceded life-forms, so imagine a place which is unfit for life, like Hades-Hadean

Using an image, tell about the three eras.

The Cenozoic, Mesozoic, and Paleozoic eras cover the same time frame as the first eon. The Mesozoic had dinosaurs and started 251 million years ago. The Paleozoic had invertebrates.

Mental image for the three eras

Picture a centurion standing next to the chart column that represents the first eon. He is grabbing the last five letters off of the name of the first eon. He is mesmerized by 25 one-dollar coins and has a pale face.

Now, apply the study methods from Step Two to choose the periods and epochs that are next to the Cenozoic Era as the next part of the geologic time scale to learn. Afterward, take a break, and then write down more observations.

Observations: Visualize the head of a centurion with a quad muscle or thigh muscle next to it, lying on the turf with air rising from it. This will remind you of the Quaternary and Tertiary Periods. Near the turf, imagine a hole with a neoprene object on the surface and something pale beneath it, representing the Neogene and Paleogene Periods as subsets of the Tertiary. Stuck with epoxy glue to the side of the quad is a halo on plywood to remind of the Holocene and Pleistocene Epochs. Stuck with epoxy glue to the side of the neoprene object is a pair of pliers pointing at me to remind you of Pliocene and Miocene Epochs. Stuck with epoxy glue to the side of the pale object is an olive on top of an egret, placed on top of a pale face to remind of the Oligocene, Eocene and Paleocene Epochs.

Now, design more flashcards using mental pictures for the periods and epochs of the first era.

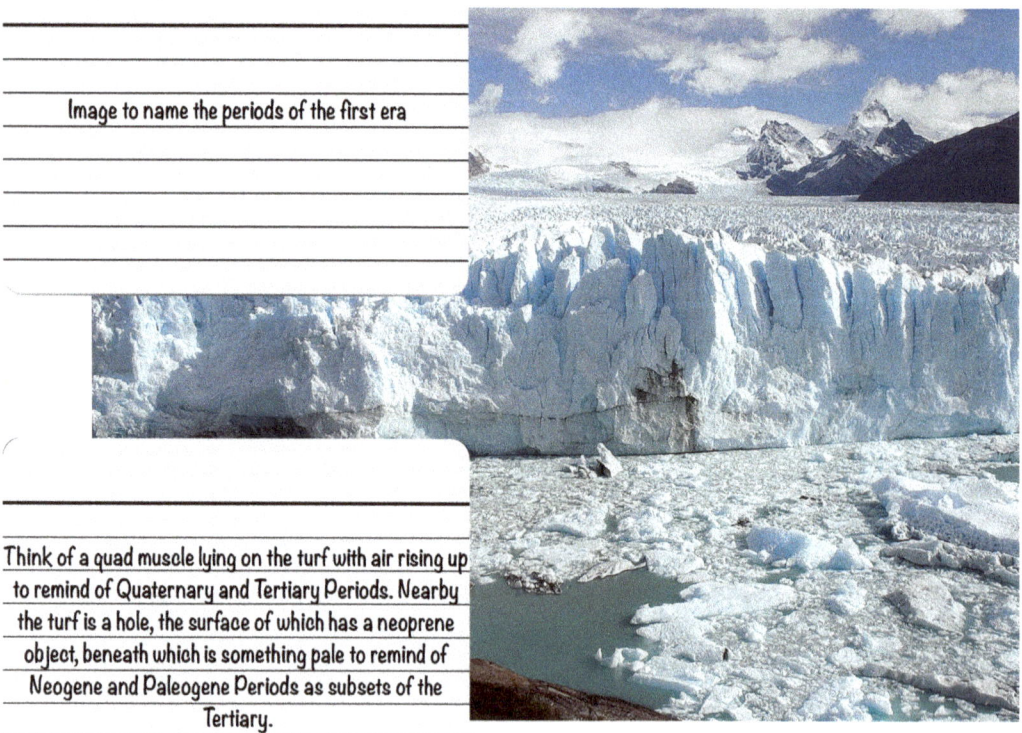

Glaciers were common during the Quaternary Period.

Image to name the periods of the first era

Think of a quad muscle lying on the turf with air rising up to remind of Quaternary and Tertiary Periods. Nearby the turf is a hole, the surface of which has a neoprene object, beneath which is something pale to remind of Neogene and Paleogene Periods as subsets of the Tertiary.

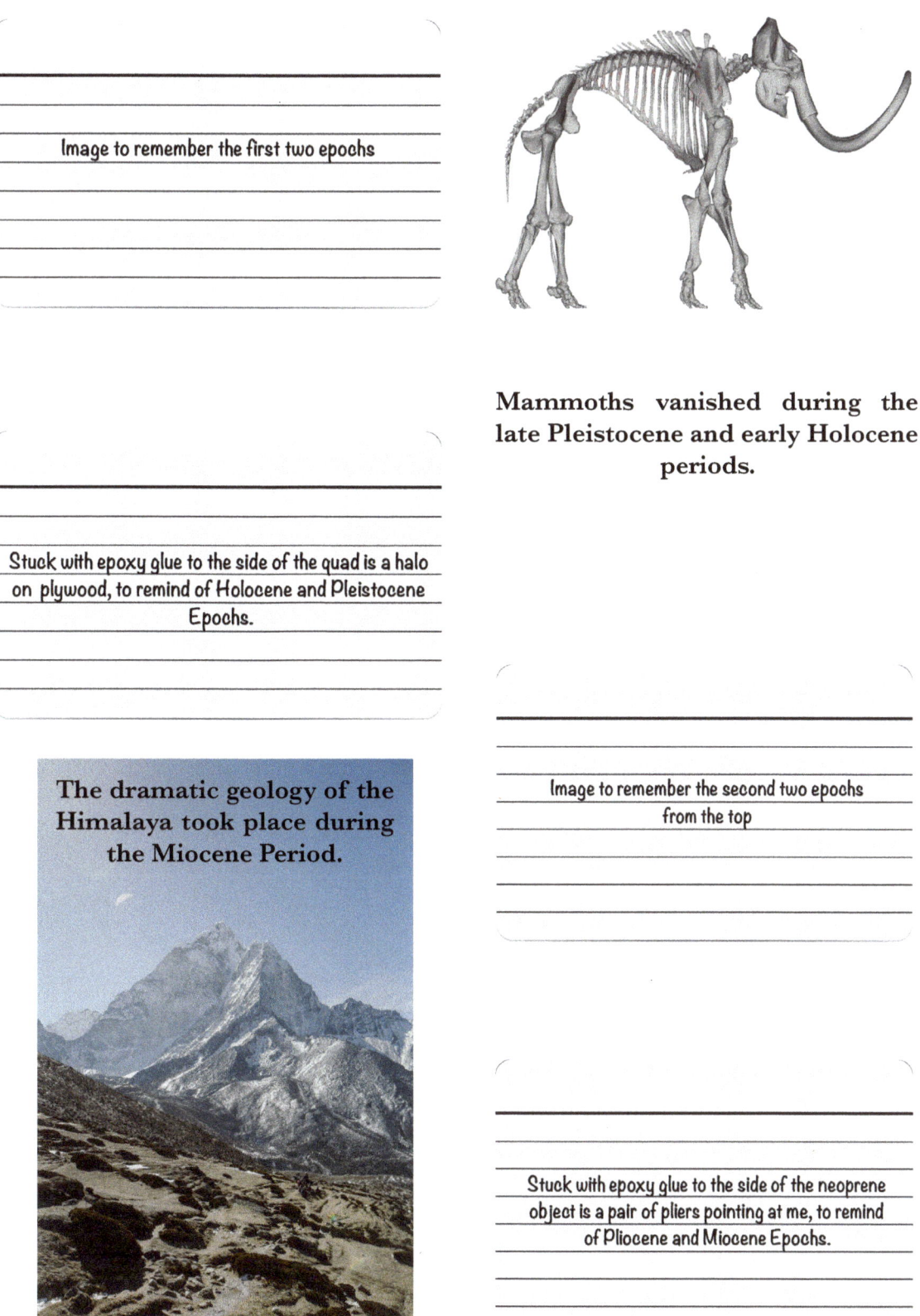

Image to remember the first two epochs

Mammoths vanished during the late Pleistocene and early Holocene periods.

Stuck with epoxy glue to the side of the quad is a halo on plywood, to remind of Holocene and Pleistocene Epochs.

The dramatic geology of the Himalaya took place during the Miocene Period.

Image to remember the second two epochs from the top

Stuck with epoxy glue to the side of the neoprene object is a pair of pliers pointing at me, to remind of Pliocene and Miocene Epochs.

Image to remember the last three epochs from the top

During the Eocene Period, forests and swamps covered the earth.

Stuck with epoxy glue to the side of the pale object is an olive on top of an egret, placed on top of a pale face to remind of the Oligocene, Eocene and Paleocene Epochs.

Step 2
Identifying Learning Objects

Gathering information is a necessary part of the studying process. Texts, lecture notes and various kinds of training sessions are sources of such information. Here are three study methods that are useful for gathering information to learn.

 Summarizing

First, in the Summarizing study method, portions of text are condensed for use in making flashcards for review and practice. Choose a manageable section of text and boil it down. If the summary contains too much information, use the Divide Big Problems study method and use other study methods to make flashcards to learn individual pieces. [In such cases, after summarizing, go back to the beginning of the Flowchart as follows: Start, Q1 – Yes, Q2 – No, Q4 – No, Q5 – Yes, S3, Q7 – Yes, Q8 – No, S7, Q8 – Yes, S6.]

Here is an example from civics:

Civics, First Amendment: (TS-6)

Summary of the First Amendment of the U. S. Constitution:

The First Amendment protects the freedom of speech, religion and the press and the right to peacefully protest and to petition the government.

 Re-reading

The second method is the reading and Re-reading study method, which offers additional exposure to a text to identify areas where you can employ other study methods described in this *Manual*. The resulting flashcards may contain important items you may have missed during the previous reading. So, to ensure you have not missed any important points, go back and search again.

 Highlighting or Underlining

The third study method to gather information is Highlighting or Underlining, which involves identifying an important fact, concept or skill.

The method can be made more effective by combining it with other study methods to create flashcards for new information. Creating and using the flashcards will engage your brain more actively and establish a consistent way to review and practice recall, thereby improving overall learning retention.

Step 3
Making Learning Objects Memorable

The next five methods are tools used for preparing information to be placed on flashcards. These methods will help you to self-administer scaffolding, enabling effective recall. You can use these tools separately or in combination to prepare information for memorization. As was already mentioned, sometimes, the result may appear unconventional, but, if it works for you, it does not have to be pretty.

 **Why Question**

The Why Question study method, also called Elaborative Interrogation in the literature, involves asking and answering Why Questions, such as "why is so and so true for this thing but not for that other thing?"

Prior knowledge is needed since familiarity with the subject is required to ask and answer why questions. Write a Why Question as a flashcard clue on one side and write the answer on the back. In some cases, one can interpret Why Question loosely, allowing questions that do not use the word "why." Look at the example on the flashcard below to understand this study method better.

Math, inequality: (TS-7)

Why does multiplying by a negative number (but not by a positive number) reverse the direction of an inequality?

Include an example.

Multiplying by a negative number changes the sign of the answer, whereas, multiplying by a positive number does not change the sign of the answer.

Inequality example: 2 < 5
Multiply by 2 yields 4 < 10
Multiply by -2 yields -4 > -10

General interest, Panama Canal: The author pondered a Why Question: why are locks needed at the Panama Canal, even though the Pacific and Atlantic Oceans are both at sea level? Answer: An Internet search (Different Viewpoint study method) revealed that Panama is mountainous, making the construction of a flat passage somewhat impractical. The canal crosses the Continental Divide at an altitude of 85 feet above sea level (Panama Canal Authority, n. d.). [Start, Q1 – Yes, Q2 – Yes, S1, Q3 – No, Q7 – Yes, Q8 – Yes, S6]

 **Self-explanation**

The Self-explanation study method is similar to certain Why Questions. Here, you attempt to explain a concept or idea, and this explanation becomes the clue or answer on the flashcard. This method is particularly helpful while solving problems, as it guides the thought process and reinforces understanding. [Start, Q1 – No, Q7 – Yes, Q8 – No, S7, Q8 – Yes, S6]

An example from sixth-grade arithmetic

Math, subtract a fraction: (TS-8)

Explain how to subtract the fraction 1/5 from the whole number 7.

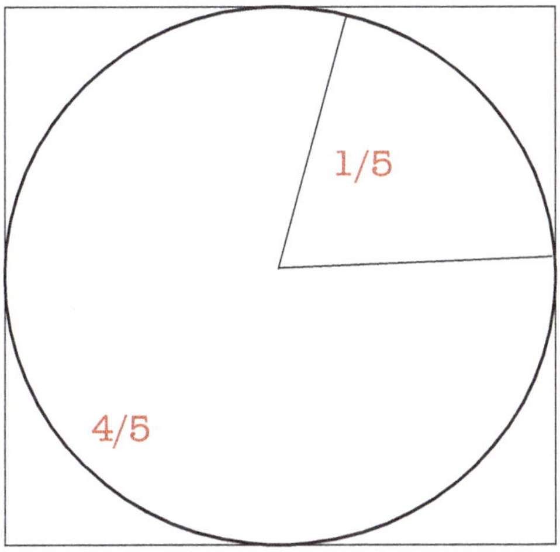

1) 7 = 6 + 1
2) 1 = 5/5
3) (6 + 5/5) - 1/5 = 6 and 4/5

If you want to learn several steps for solving a special type of problem, try the Divide Big Problems study method. Group the steps chronologically and memorize them using various study methods and flashcards.

Chess: After researching the game, describe the common opening for a chess game, called the Queen's Gambit, where the player moving the white pieces goes first, and the queen's pawn must advance two spaces. What strategy will this flashcard use? *Self-explanation.*

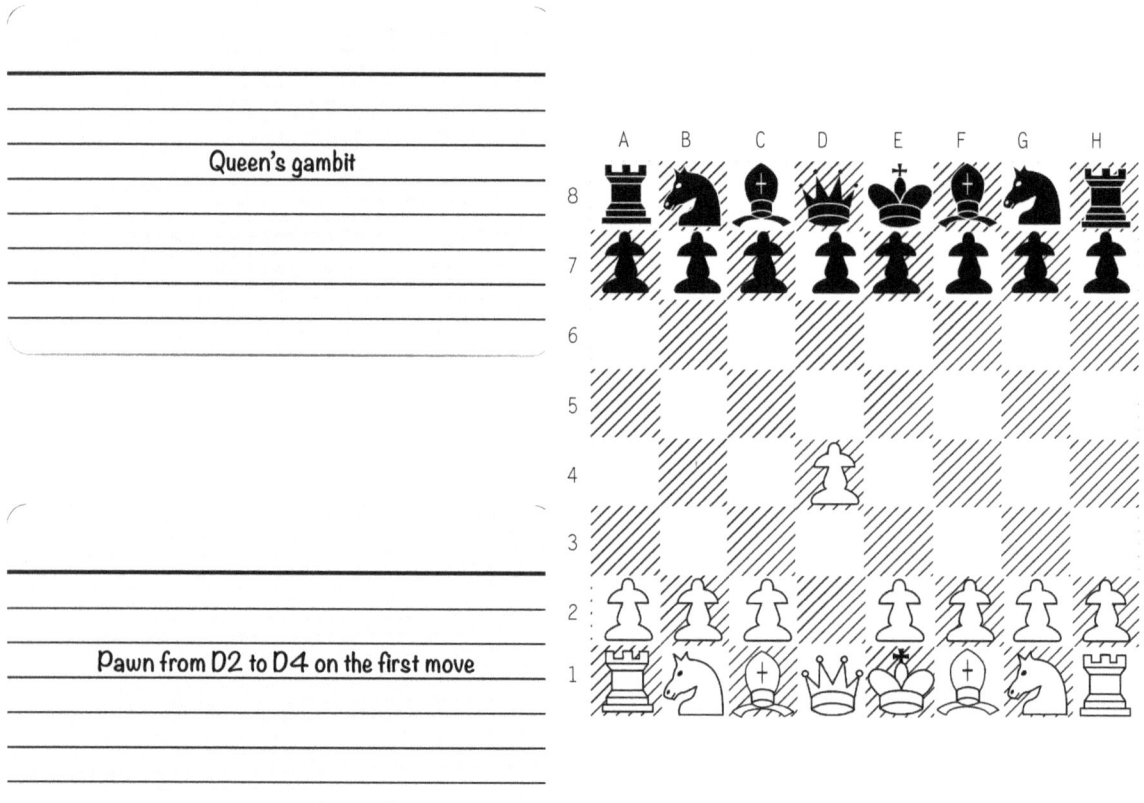

Queen's gambit

Pawn from D2 to D4 on the first move

Now, watch a YouTube demo of a chess situation called Fool's Mate. Then, describe it from memory as follows: In the first two moves, the player moving the white pieces advances one pawn to F3 or F4 and another pawn to G4. The player moving the black pieces advances a pawn to E6 or E5 on the first move and the queen to H4 for a two-move checkmate on the second turn! Flashcards for these facts will utilize the Self-explanation study method.

Fool's mate

White's first two moves include one pawn to F3 or F4 and another to G4. Black's first move is a pawn to E6 or E5, and second move is queen to H4 for a two-move checkmate.

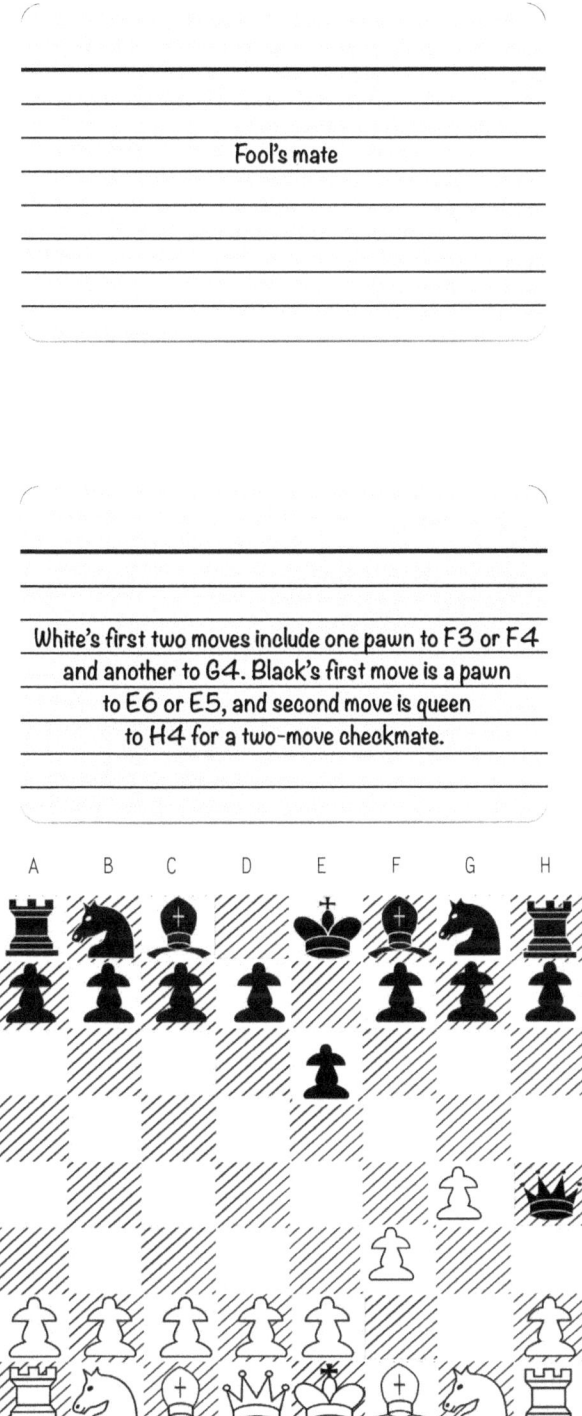

Continue to study other famous chess situations, making flashcards for review and practice.

Keyword or Mnemonic

Third, in the Keyword or Mnemonic study method, you utilize a word, phrase or symbol as a clue to recall a fact, concept or skill. These cues act as mental pegs on which to hang information. In this first example, the flashcard demonstrates that you can make your memory clue personal since it only has to work for you. See the author's example below.

Example from Physics

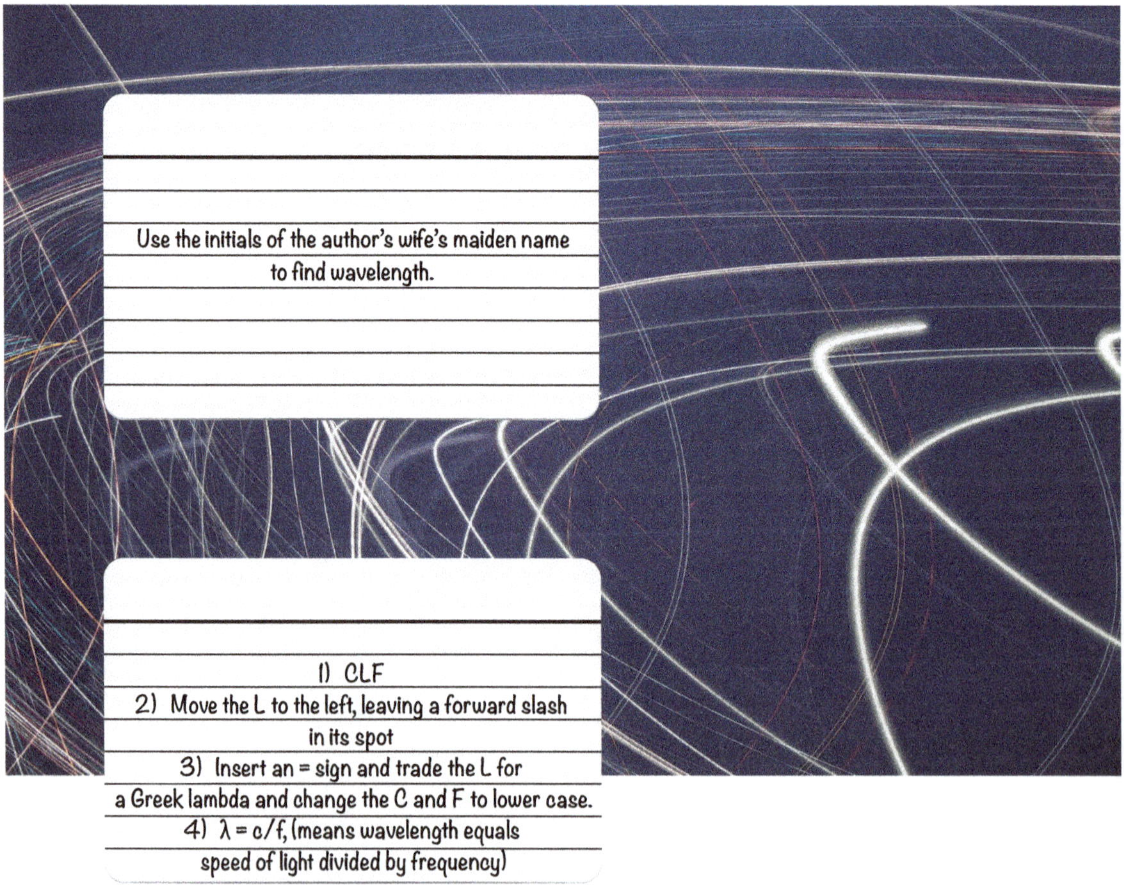

Use the initials of the author's wife's maiden name to find wavelength.

1) CLF
2) Move the L to the left, leaving a forward slash in its spot
3) Insert an = sign and trade the L for a Greek lambda and change the C and F to lower case.
4) $\lambda = c/f$, (means wavelength equals speed of light divided by frequency)

Algebra, circle: (TS-3) The Keyword or Mnemonic study method can be useful for our earlier discussions about circles and similar learning objects becoming confusing. As you will likely recall, these two flashcards were studied and practice-tested together to notice slight differences and thus avoid confusing them with one another.

We need to make our brain connect *circumference* with *2* and *area* with *squared*. Two and table start with "t," so we could use circumference to remind us of a table using a joke: Who designed and built King Arthur's table? Sir Cumference.

Now, we need to connect *area* with *squared*. Since area can be expressed in square feet, the following flashcards using these cues could be useful:

Algebra, order of operations: (TS-9) When learning the order of operations, list the operations in decreasing order and then revisit Step Three to find a way to remember the order of operations: parentheses, power, multiply or divide, and add or subtract. Look for a pattern in the words to use the Keyword or Mnemonic study method. Notice the word "parent" in the word parenthesis, which could be a keyword to remind you of the first operation.

Here is an attempt to create a mental image to remember the keywords: "parents" have the power to multiply (or divide in the case of an amoeba) and add to or subtract from your allowance. A flashcard could then be created with this information:

> Order of operations
> (an image using keywords)

> Parents have the power to multiply (or to divide in the case of an amoeba) and to add to your allowance or subtract from it.

> Explain how to use the order of operations in a problem.
>
> (Use an image of keywords.)

Another flashcard could use the Self-explanation study method to show what the image means.

> First, perform operations inside of the parentheses. Then, perform the power operations, if any, multiply or divide, and finally, add or subtract.

Now, employ the Learner-Generated Scenario study method from Step Five to practice problem-solving. Create and solve some easy problems that use different combinations of the order of operations.

Chemistry, diatomic gasses: (TS-10) The Keyword or Mnemonic study method can help in remembering the elements that form diatomic gasses. Arrange the symbols of the elements such that they spell a word. For example, Br, I, Cl, F, H, O and N sound like "brickle phone." Now, imagine a phone shaped like a brick on one end and like a pickle on the other to form a mental image of the word. When we remove the k and the e's and change the p to an f, we now have "briclfhon" or Br, I, Cl, F, H, O, N. We can now create flashcards for effective memorization.

Explain how to remember the diatomic gasses.

(Use the Keyword or Mnemonic study method.)

Imagine a phone that is half brick and half pickle, namely, "bricklephone," then remove the k and e's and change the p to an f, yielding "briclfhon."

Br, I, Cl, F, H, O, N

Calculus, parts equation: (TS-11) If you want to recall how the equation for the integration by parts procedure begins, look at the equation $\int u\, dv = uv - \int v\, du$. Remember where the integral symbols and "d" letters are and remove them, to be re-inserted later. Memorize the order of the equal sign and the minus sign and remove them, to be re-inserted later. That leaves us with the following:

$$u\ v \quad u\ v \quad v\ u$$

Using the Keyword or Mnemonic study method from Step Three, you may notice that the equation uses the abbreviation for ultraviolet light—UV. These two letters are repeated and then reversed.

The north pole of Jupiter as seen in ultraviolet light	Meaning of integration by parts equation clues:
	1. ultraviolet
	2. order
	3. signs
	4. dd
	5. integral

	1. u v
	2. Repeat, then reverse the letters.
	3. Re-insert the = and the −
	4. Re-insert d's in-between both first and last pairs of letters.
	5. Re-insert the integral signs at the start of the first and last pairs of letters.

Put together, the clues are ultraviolet, order, signs, dd and integral.
You could include the Mental Imagery study method by imagining a vivid scene or mental picture to remind you of the learning object.

Image to remember the integration by parts equation

Ultraviolet sunlight is streaming through a window into a courtroom, where a judge is pounding with a gavel to get order. The people in the courtroom are carrying signs. The signs have the letter d on them. Courts need integrity. Take off the last three letters of integrity and add "al."

Recite the integration by parts equation.

(Use a Mental Image and Keywords or Mnemonics.)

$$\int u\, dv = uv - \int v\, du$$

 **Mental Imagery**

The Mental Imagery study method involves forming a mental picture while reading or listening to a text. Instead of reading for yourself, it is somewhat better when another person reads to you, because the reading process itself interferes and can make this method difficult. An unusual mind picture can be especially memorable.

By the way, in this method, sketching the mental image with a pen or pencil has been found actually detrimental to learning, so a brief written description of the mental picture could be used as the answer or clue on a flashcard. An added benefit for a person reading aloud is brain stimulation (Nouchi, 2012).

Literature, moral: (TS-12)

Moral from the Les Misérables: priest's forgiveness of Jean Valjean
(Use a mental image.)

The image of police bringing Jean Valjean and the stolen silver candlesticks to the priest's door, only to have the priest say they are a gift, illustrates a heroic act of kindness.

Chemistry, diatomic gasses: (TS-10) Let us choose the diatomic gasses, alkali metals, alkali earth metals, common halogens and common noble gasses to study, and form a mental image from studying the periodic table. The diatomic gasses include H, N, O, F, Cl, Br and I. Notice that, if you start with the upper-most and left-most element, and then look for the word "NO" to begin an upside-down and backwards "L," the periodic table itself provides the needed list. The other chosen groupings are facts that are ready for Step Four. We will cover them later.

Explain how to use the periodic table to find the seven diatomic gasses.

(Use a mental image.)

↓

Pick the upper-most and left-most element, look for and choose the word "NO" and make an upside-down and backwards "L," by bending down from the top of the halogens until you have selected all seven elements.

Looking at the periodic table, list the diatomic elements.

(Use a mental image.)

↓

$H_2, N_2, O_2, F_2, Cl_2, Br_2, I_2$

Chemistry, pouring order: (TS-13) When diluting a strong acid or base, knowing the pouring order of chemicals is important to prevent a sudden explosive reaction. To remember how to pour chemicals safely, use the Mental Imagery study method from Step Three. First, visualize the incorrect way of pouring a little water into a strong acid or base, where the water is surrounded by a dangerous chemical. If, instead, you correctly add a small amount of strong acid or base to water, each unit of concentrated acid or base will be surrounded by water, making it dilute and safe.

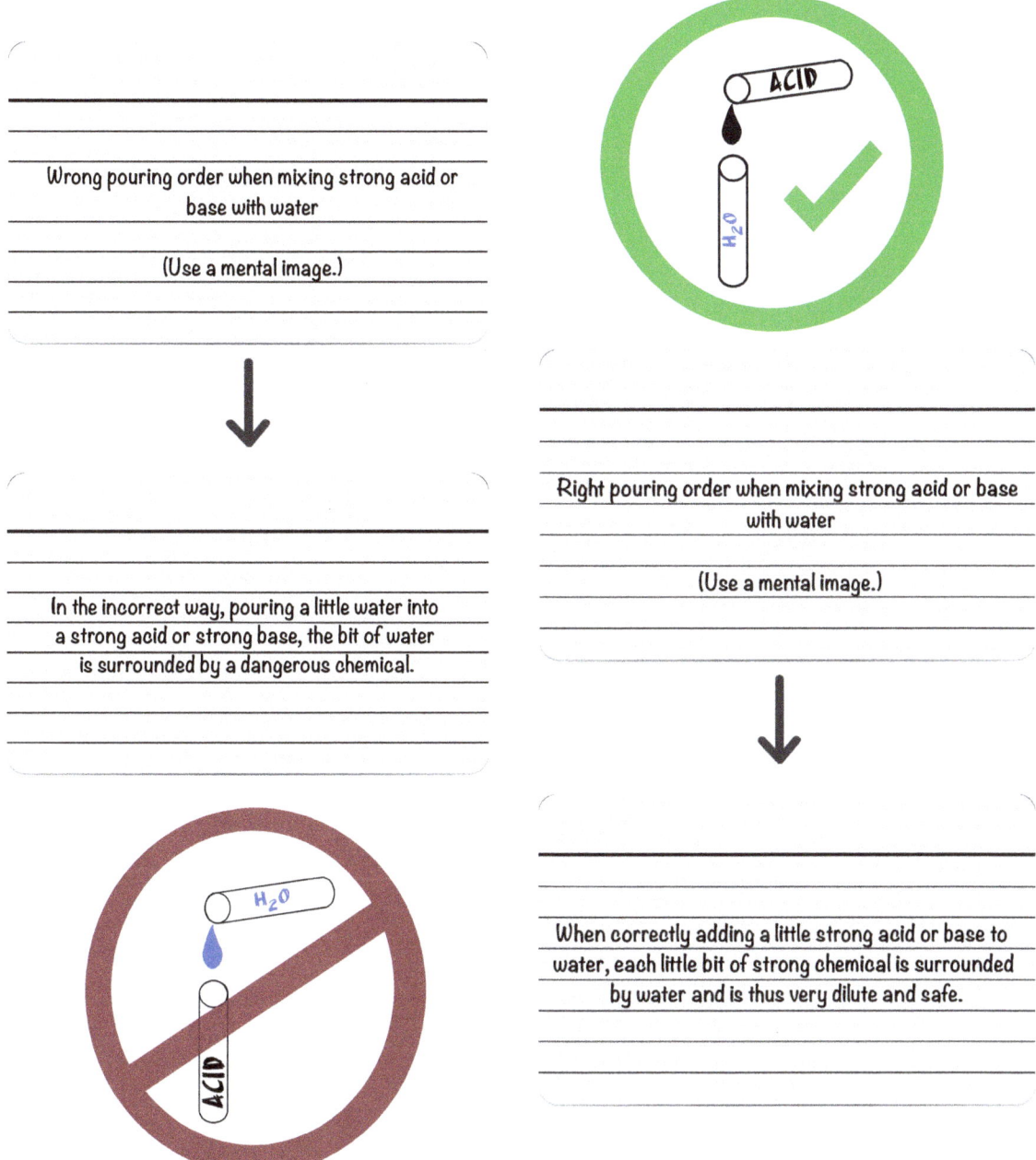

Geology, hardness scale: (TS-14) When learning to identify minerals, a unique characteristic to remember is their hardness, which, along with other characteristics such as the streak, forms a type of fingerprint.

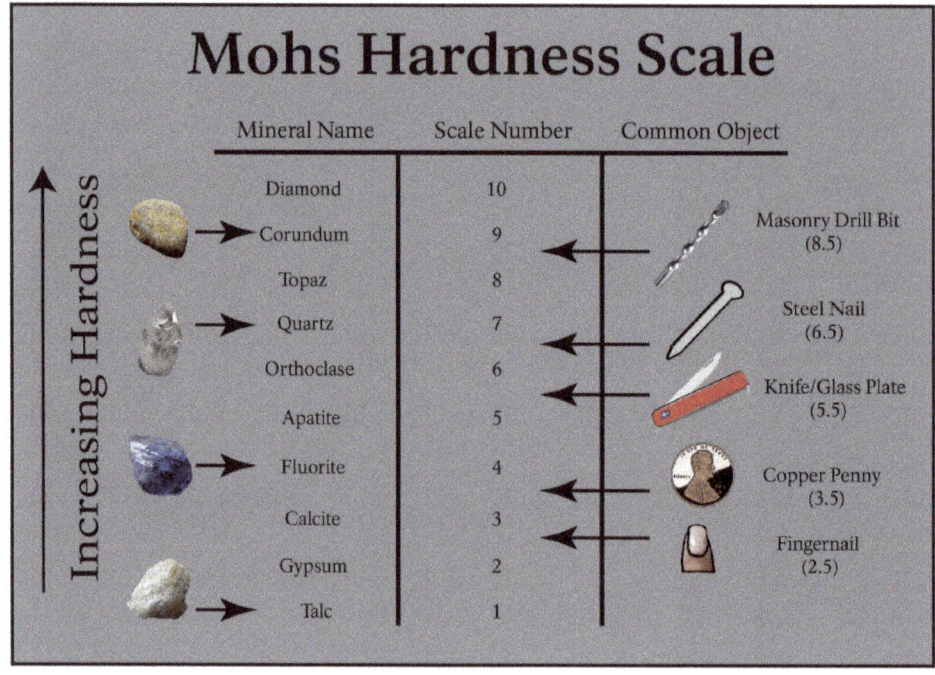

To remember the ten standard minerals on the Mohs hardness scale (National Park Service, 2018), use an unusual memorization order. Pair the softest and hardest minerals first, followed by the next softest and next hardest and so on. After following this method, the following pairs will be formed: talc and diamond (one and ten), gypsum and corundum (two and nine), calcite and topaz (three and eight), fluorite and quartz (four and seven) and apatite and orthoclase (five and six).

Then, combine the Keyword or Mnemonic study method and the Mental Imagery study method to create an image connecting similar words to remind you of the names of the minerals on the scale. For example, talcum powder on a diamond ring on a Gypsy was a conundrum for a man with a calculator and a toupee, with fluoride on a quartz watch and with an appetite for food from an orthogonal case.

To check whether your recall is correct, write down the numbers from one to ten and, using the mental image for clues, write down the minerals as per their hardness. It should give the following result:

10 Diamond
9 Corundum
8 Topaz
7 Quartz
6 Orthoclase
5 Apatite
4 Fluorite
3 Calcite
2 Gypsum
1 Talc

Gypsum Crystals: 2 on the Mohs Hardness Scale

Since the part about the man has a lot to remember, it could use an enhanced image, so as to remember it better, for example the following: "…for a man with a calculator, wearing a toupee for a beard and biting down with fluoride-treated teeth onto a quartz watch, because of an appetite, by which he opens an orthogonal case holding food." [In terms of following the Flowchart, you are at S7 and follow the arrow to Q8 – Yes, S6, S8, Q8. The answer to Q8 is No, so you return to S7 and design the enhancement.]

Now practice by describing the image again from memory and then repeating the items from the list. The following flashcards are an example.

Blue Topaz: 8 on the Mohs Hardness Scale

Gary Dean Petersen

Describe a mental image for recalling standard minerals from the Mohs scale

Diamond: 10 on the Mohs Hardness Scale

Talcum powder on a diamond ring on a Gypsy was a conundrum for a man with a calculator and a toupee and with fluoride on a quartz watch and with an appetite for food from an orthogonal case.

Using a mental image, recall a list of minerals on the Mohs hardness scale.

Calcite: 3 on the Mohs Hardness Scale

10 diamond	5 apatite
9 corundum	4 flourite
8 topaz	3 calcite
7 quartz	2 gypsum
6 orthoclase	1 talc

Poker: (TS-15) To remember which hand beats the other in poker, use the study methods by first finding a list from highest to lowest (Fortune Palace, n. d.): royal flush, straight flush, four of a kind, full house, flush, straight, three of a kind, two pair, pair, high card. To proceed, use both the Keyword or Mnemonic study method and the Mental Imagery study method from Step Three. Then, use the Learner-Generated Scenario study method from Step Five to obtain a simulated experience as a poker player. Thus, you can create a mental image to remember the list.

Image of what beats what in poker

King flipping a toilet lever, the unbent pipe carries a straight flush; nearby, four identical plumbers are needed because of a full house of backed up problem, they get a flush, straight away, using three plungers, two pair of boots and one pair of gloves that are holding a playing card up in the air

Royal Flush

Using a mental image, list possible poker hands from highest to lowest.

Royal flush, straight flush, four of a kind, full house, flush, straight, three of a kind, two pair, pair and high card

Next, apply what you have learned to understand and retain the information more effectively. Imagine a poker game with several players, and determine the winner based on hand rankings to find the highest hand.

Then, imagine what would happen in a scenario where two players have four of a kind. Jacks beat Deuces, but what if two or more players have a full house? Would the one having the higher ranking three cards of a kind in the full house win? To find out, use the Different Viewpoint study method from Step One by checking a reference to determine if you are right.

Another possible scenario would be two players holding two pairs. If they are the same two pairs, the fifth card could decide the winner. But what if the fifth card is also of the same value? Perhaps they would draw for a higher card to decide or arm wrestle for it? Going through other scenarios that could happen in a game will help you grow more proficient, just as drawing practice would have helped an Old West gunslinger prepare for a gunfight.

Civics, First Amendment: (TS-6) As you may recall, we used a civics example for the Summarizing study method. The summary of the First Amendment of the Constitution of the United States of America is repeated below.

The First Amendment protects the freedom of speech, religion and the press and the right to peacefully protest and petition the government.

Let us now design a way to memorize the points of the summary. We can use the Mental Imagery study method from Step Three to do this.

Next, jot down the keywords and create mental image to remember them. For example:

A) three pictures for speech, religion, and press;
and
B) two pictures for peacefully protest and petitioning the government.

Now create the flashcards. [Since, at this point, we have already decided on two sets of images, the Flowchart reasoning would be as follows: Start, Q1 – No, Q7 – Yes, Q8 – No, S7, Q8 – Yes, S6.]

Mental image to recall Part A of the rights the First Amendment protects

Three pictures:
First, imagine a newspaper (for press) being read someone with a large mouth where the head should be (for speech) and wearing a cross necklace (for religion).

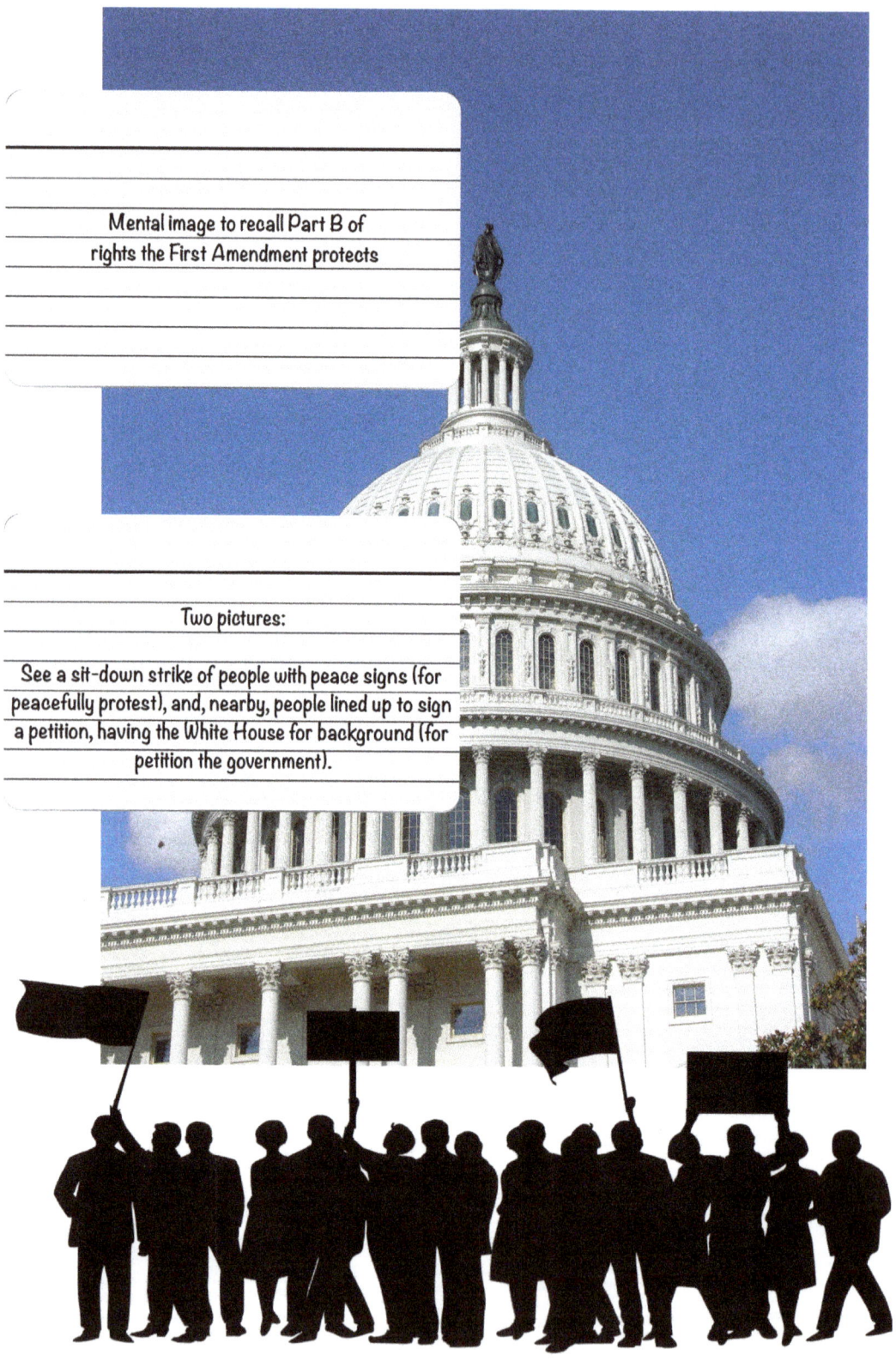

Mental image to recall Part B of rights the First Amendment protects

Two pictures:

See a sit-down strike of people with peace signs (for peacefully protest), and, nearby, people lined up to sign a petition, having the White House for background (for petition the government).

Geography, Central America: (TS-16) To learn the names of the countries in Central America, make a list by studying a map (Sawe, 2016).

The list includes Belize, Guatemala, Honduras, El Salvador, Nicaragua, Costa Rica and Panama. Try using similar-sounding hints for the Keyword or Mnemonic study method in step three. For example, bell lease, guacamole, Honda, saliva, nicotine, coast and Pan Am. Now, use the Mental Imagery study method to visualize a picture of a Taco Bell (for) lease that is advertising guacamole. In front is the owner, sitting on a Honda and chewing tobacco. His saliva contains nicotine. He's headed to the coast to catch a Pan Am flight.

Gary Dean Petersen

The Flags of Central America

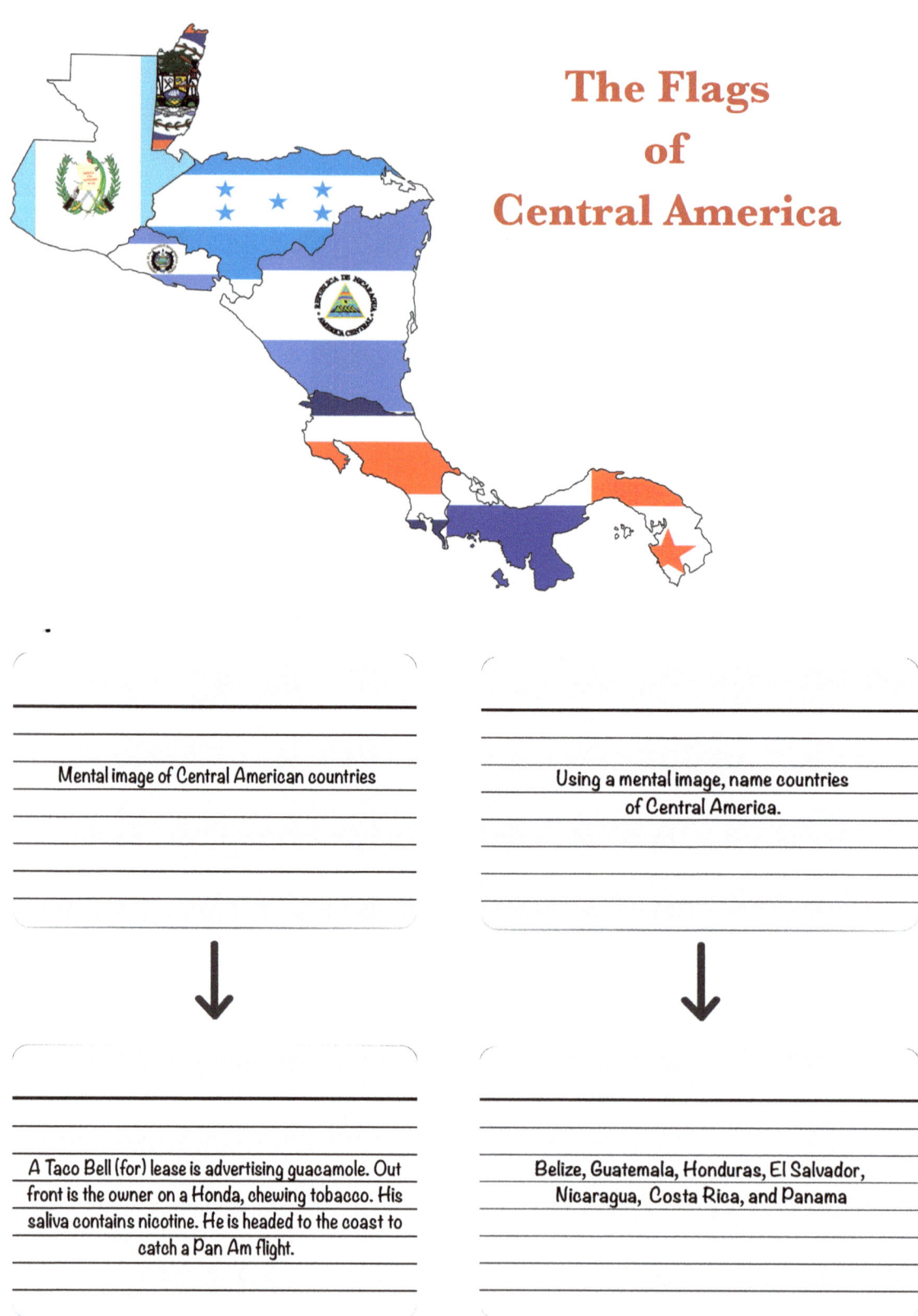

Mental image of Central American countries

↓

A Taco Bell (for) lease is advertising guacamole. Out front is the owner on a Honda, chewing tobacco. His saliva contains nicotine. He is headed to the coast to catch a Pan Am flight.

Using a mental image, name countries of Central America.

↓

Belize, Guatemala, Honduras, El Salvador, Nicaragua, Costa Rica, and Panama

 **Simple as Pie**

Finally, the fifth study method of Step Three is called Simple as Pie, where we attempt to simplify complex items, such as in a math problem, with an analogy. For example, 0.75 times y is 0.75 of a pie or ¾ of an apple pie. Sometimes, using such a visual aid can clarify the problem, make it simpler, and provide a sensible method to check how reasonable an answer is. Thus, when the learning objective can be modeled or appears complicated, an analogy could help.

Chemistry, pouring order: (TS-13) Since safety is highly important, let us develop a second method for remembering the pouring order. Using the Simple as Pie study method, we can develop an analogy. For example, pouring into something is akin to diving into something. Diving into dangerous chemicals sounds unsafe, whereas diving into water sounds safe. Make flashcards to reinforce this idea.

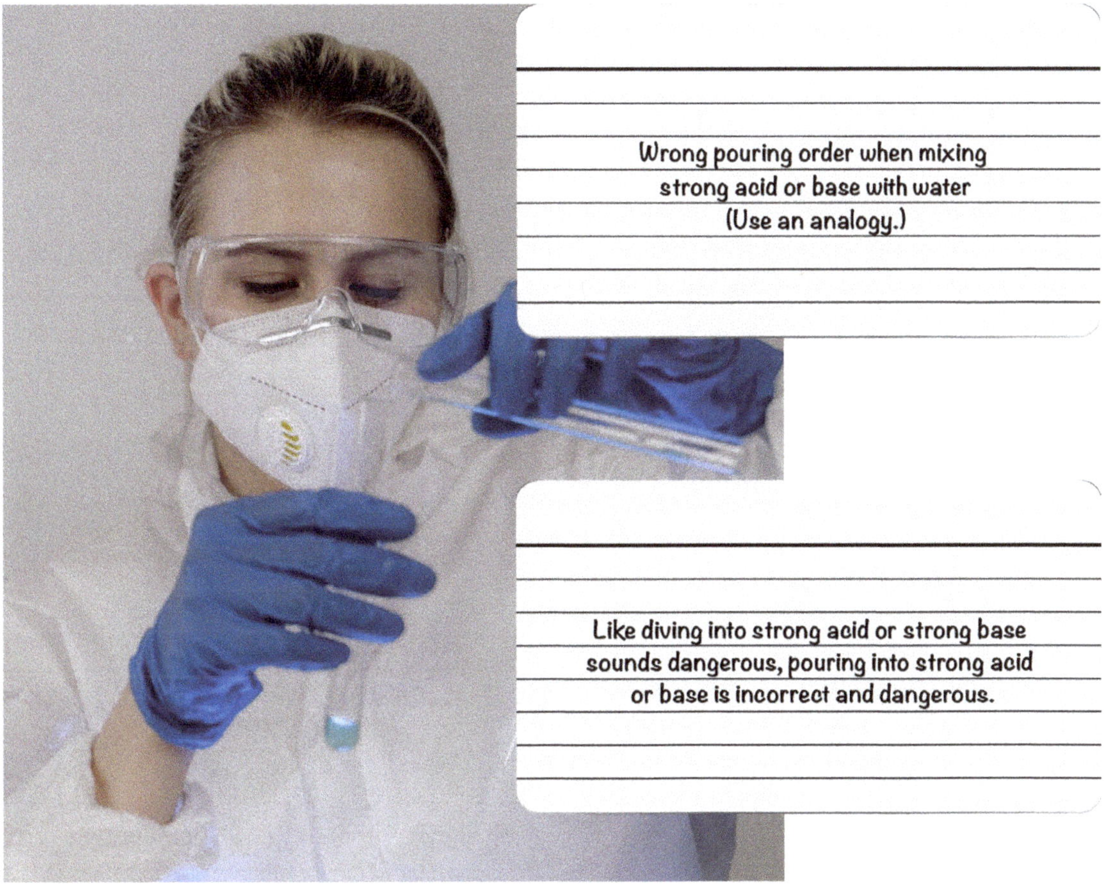

> Wrong pouring order when mixing strong acid or base with water (Use an analogy.)

> Like diving into strong acid or strong base sounds dangerous, pouring into strong acid or base is incorrect and dangerous.

Right pouring order when mixing strong acid or base with water (Use an analogy.)

Like diving into water sounds safe, pouring into water is safe, so the right way to dilute is to pour into water.

Chemistry, single replacement reaction: (TS-17) Simple replacement is another type of chemical reaction. Use the Simple as Pie study method from Step One to create an analogy that will help you identify a simple replacement reaction as follows.

Christmas tree + present → Christmas present + tree.

Simple replacement reaction

As you check your work with examples of acid reacting with metal, you may find that this analogy is flawed because in the equation $2HCl + 2K \rightarrow 2KCl + H_2$, which—since the metal cation (positively charged ion) is listed first after the arrow by convention—would yield the less satisfying result: "Christmas tree + present → present tree + Christmas." So, make a different analogy that works. The extra thinking may assist recall. The following would be a better analogy:

$2HCl_{(aq)} + 2K_{(s)} \rightarrow 2KCl_{(aq)} + H_{2(g)}$

reaction type

Simple replacement reaction

After answering, you could check to see if the graph-paper-and-notebook analogy works.

$2HCl + 2K \rightarrow 2KCl + H_2$.

Here, "graph" stands for H, "paper" stands for Cl and "notebook" stands for K. So, it correctly says "graph paper + notebook ➔ notebook paper + graph." This may seem like extra work, but when you are taking an exam in class, won't it feel great to prove to yourself that you have gotten that answer right?

+

Step 4
Practicing Recalling Objects

The next two study methods cover some details on how to form and use flashcards. Once a fact, concept or skill has been identified as ready to commit to memory, a flashcard can be made.

 **Practice Testing**

The Practice Testing study method, which is inexorably linked with the Delayed Testing study method in this *Manual*, involves using a clue to practice recalling information. A good way to execute Practice Testing is by using flashcards.

To start, select a group of flashcards with the question or clue side facing you. Then, go through the flashcards one by one, attempting to recall the answer on the other side. Place the flashcards that you recall correctly in one stack and the difficult-to-recall ones in another stack to study for a later retest.

Science: Facts are frequently ready for flashcards, so you can skip to Step Four of the study methods. Interesting science facts, such as information about insects, are generally ready to be placed on flashcards.

How do you tell a moth from a butterfly?

A moth antenna looks like a feather, while a butterfly antenna looks like a stick with a ball on the end.

Describe an insect leg joint.

It is similar to a ball in a socket so it can rotate. Hold a fist with the other hand and turn the fist.

Where are the holes for insects to breathe?

On the sides of the body

What is different about a grasshopper chewing and a person chewing?

Insect jaws close from the sides of the mouth toward the middle, not up and down like people's mouths.

Spelling: More than one study method can be applied when learning how to spell words. Children are often introduced to new, flashcard-ready vocabulary words while learning to spell. Two fourth-grade level spelling words, desire and glance, are shown here as examples. Using the Practice Testing study method of Step Four, create flashcards with the words on one side and their meanings on the other side.

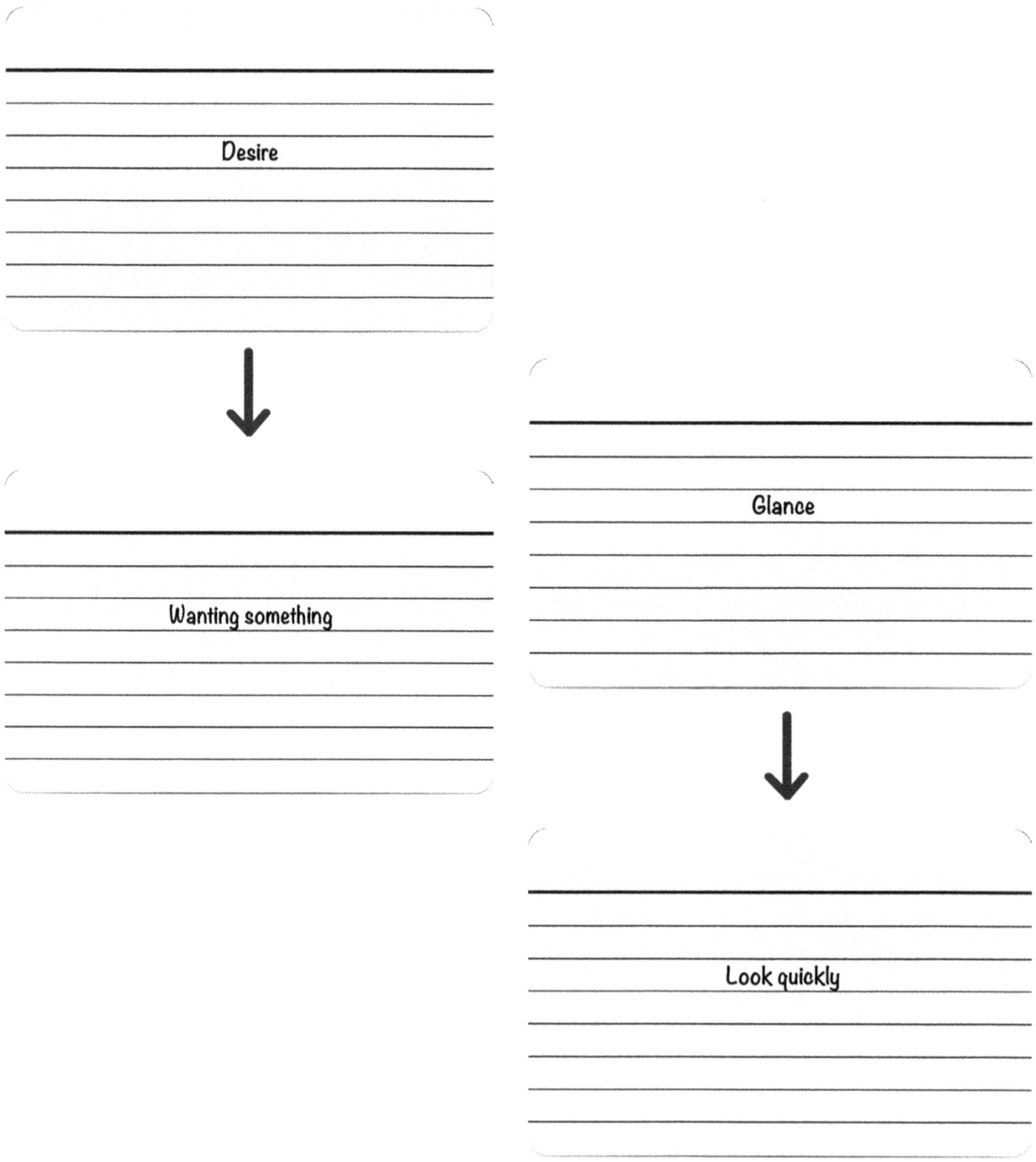

Desire

↓

Wanting something

Glance

↓

Look quickly

Students can practice with the flashcards until they know the meanings of the words. The ability to associate words with their meanings is useful for later self-testing.

Next is Step Five, where students can improve their recall of the spelling words by employing the Learner-Generated Scenario study method. One effective approach is to write sentences that correctly use the spelling words. An actual student wrote, "I desire Ryan. I glance at him." Then, to practice for their spelling test, students can return to Step Four, Practicing Recalling Objects, and turn over all the flashcards so that the meanings are on the top and the spelling words are on the bottom. Now, with a piece of paper and a pencil, the students can give themselves a practice spelling test by looking at the meaning and then spelling the corresponding word. Care should be taken not to peek at the answers until the test is finished.

Then, the students can review the answers and grade their performance. If any answers are incorrect, the students should study them and then wait for a few hours or days (Delayed Testing study method) before taking another practice test. This time gap allows the students' brains to build memories.

Using a children's dictionary, the students can choose some extra spelling words to learn. Such dedication to learning is commendable and will make them great students!

Chemistry, periodic table: Some periodic table facts are already ready to be applied to flashcards. The alkali metals and each one's atomic number, symbol and approximate atomic mass include lithium 3, Li, 7; sodium 11, Na, 23; potassium 19, K, 39; rubidium 37, Rb, 85.5; cesium 55, Cs, 133; and francium 87, Fr, 223; all of which tend to lose one valence electron to be similar to the noble gas of the previous row, leaving a positive charge. Create flashcards with the name as the clue on one side and the atomic number, symbol and approximate mass on the other. One example of an alkali metal flashcard follows, along with another flashcard with the usual charge acquired by the group.

Alkali metal
Lithium: number, symbol and approximate mass

Lithium floating in oil

3
Li
7

What is the usual charge of an alkali metal?

Lithium Carbonate

Positive one

The alkali earth metals and their atomic numbers, symbols and approximate masses are as follows: beryllium 4, Be, 9; magnesium 12, Mg, 24; calcium 20, Ca, 40; strontium 38, Sr, 87.6; barium 56, Ba, 137 and radium 88, Ra, 226. An example of an alkali earth flashcard is given below, along with another flashcard bearing the usual charge of an ion in the group.

Alkali earth metal
beryllium: number, symbol and approximate mass

Beryllium

4
Be
9

What is the usual charge of an alkali earth metal?

Barium

Positive two

The common halogens are fluorine 9, F, 19; chlorine 17, Cl, 35.5; bromine 35, Br, 80 and iodine 53, I, 127. They tend to gain one electron to be similar to the nearest noble gas. Create flashcards with the name on one side and the atomic number, symbol and approximate mass on the other. An example flashcard for the common halogens is given below, along with one bearing the usual charge of an ion in the group.

Halogen
fluorine: number, symbol and approximate mass

9
F
Fluorine
18.998403

17
Cl
Chlorine
35.4527

35
Br
Bromine
79.904

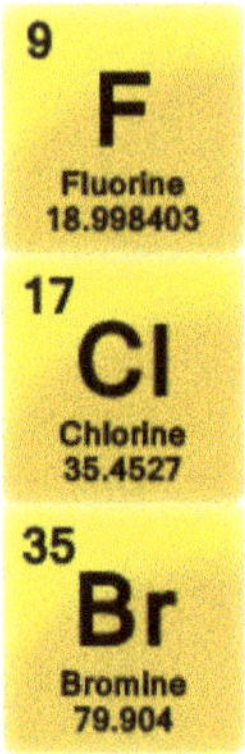

9
F
19

What is the usual charge of a halogen?

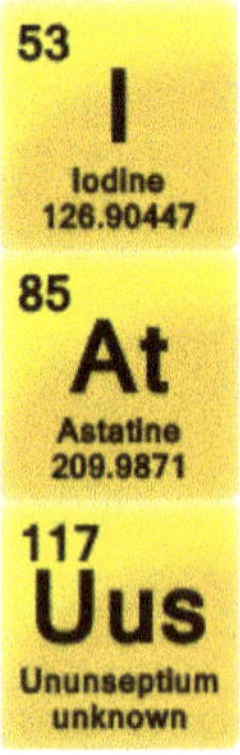

53
I
Iodine
126.90447

85
At
Astatine
209.9871

117
Uus
Ununseptium
unknown

Negative one

The common noble gasses are helium 2, He, 4; neon 10, Ne, 20; argon 18, Ar, 40; krypton 36, Kr, 84; xenon 54, Xe, 131 and radon 86, Rn, 222. Create flashcards with the name on one side and the atomic number, symbol and approximate mass on the other. An example flashcard for the noble gases is given below, along with a flashcard bearing the usual charge taken on elements in this group.

Noble gasses
helium: number, symbol and approximate mass

Liquified Helium

2
He
4

What is the usual charge of a noble gas?

Xenon

Zero

Physics: To remember that a high center of gravity is less stable than a low center of gravity, visualize two people wrestling, and the opponents (unlike in the picture below) place one foot together and then, while holding one hand, try to overpower the other to make the loser move his back foot. In the image, visualize the shorter wrestler win due to a lower center of gravity. You could practice recalling the image by using a flashcard.

Boxing, rabbit punch: (TS-18) To learn the meaning of several boxing terms, you could use the Different Viewpoint study methods by researching rabbit punch (Miriam-Webster, n. d.), kidney punch (Garland, 2019), sucker punch (Miriam-Webster, n. d.) and glass jaw (Miriam-Webster, n. d.) on the Internet. Create flashcards with simple definitions and use the Practice Testing study method under Step Four. Vocabulary words are frequently ready for flashcards without other methods.

Rabbit punch

↓

A short chopping blow to the back of the neck or the base of the skull

Kidney punch

↓

A punch on the back, near the elbow

Sucker punch

A sudden punch with no warning (and usually unprovoked)

Glass jaw

Being easy prey for a knockout punch

 **Delayed Testing**

In the Delayed Testing study method (also known as distributed practice), learners deliberately introduce a delay of several hours or days between studying flashcards and reviewing them for recall. The delay allows the brain enough time to form the connections required for recall.

This method does not generate flashcards but rather is a timing strategy. Without the delay, the flashcards may seem less useful until the brain has had time to develop essential memories (Dunlosky et al., 2013).

Step 5
Applying Learning Objects

 **Learner-Generated Scenario**

The Learner-Generated Scenario study method involves learners actively creating situations or problems to solve using the facts, concepts or skills they wish to learn. Engaging in this dynamic brain activity helps to apply the learning object memorably and possibly generate new related learning objects as a spinoff. Practicing with scenarios or problems should be done often to master learning objects. If, during this study method, a new learning objective is generated that is neither ready for memorization nor to be made memorable, the learner should revisit the Decision Tree to develop a proper plan to learn that objective.

Chemistry, reactions: When reading about hydrocarbon combustion reactions in a high school chemistry textbook (Wilbraham, 2002), several facts are ready to learn. For example, hydrocarbons contain H and C. Combustion combines them with O_2. A complete burn yields H_2O and CO_2. An incomplete burn can also yield C. The human body uses slow combustion as a source of energy.

To effectively process this information, combine the Mental Imagery study method with the Why Question study method from Step Three and the Learner-Generated Scenario study method from Step Five as follows:

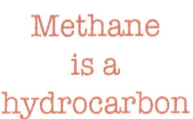
Methane is a hydrocarbon

One image could be the snuffing of a candle causing smoke.

Why does snuffing out a candle cause smoke?

Smoke likely has carbon in it, because the burn is no longer complete.

Why does burning oil make black smoke?

The oil is combusting incompletely, and so the smoke contains carbon.

For another example, imagine a vehicle with worn valves burning oil and producing black smoke from its exhaust pipe.

> Why do mouths breathe out little clouds on cold days?

> Burning hydrocarbons yields H_2O and CO_2.

Use the Different Viewpoint study method to double-check your answers about clouds (Dunbar, 2015). [Since there is uncertainty about the cloud answers, some confusion is present. So, to follow the reasoning of the Flowchart, go back to the beginning as follows: [Start, Q1 – Yes, Q2 – Yes, S1, Q3 – No, Q7 – Yes, Q8 – Yes, S6.] Another image that may come to mind is a tailpipe dripping moisture.

Why does a tailpipe sometimes drip moisture?

Water from combustion is cooling and condensing in the pipe.

Why do tailpipes sometimes not drip moisture?

The water is hot, uncondensed vapor.

Yet another image could be pictures of a person before and after losing weight.

Chemistry, uric acid: (TS-19) A student learns that bat guano and bird droppings contain uric acid (Nature's Crusaders, 2009), and gout is a joint disease where uric acid is present in joints. A teacher hears the student claim that gout is bird manure in the joints. Using from Step One, Different Viewpoint study method, the student learns from the teacher that birds do not put droppings on joints.

Result: The student uses the Step Three, Why Question study method and the Step Five, Learner-Generated Scenario study method to consider the following question:

> **Why do birds shed nitrogen as solid, while most animals use liquid?**

> Liquid weighs more.
> Birds need to be lightweight to fly.

Using the Internet, find structures of uric acid and urea to explore their solubility in water. The results of the research on both structures are shown below.

The structure of uric acid (National Center for Biotechnology, n. d.) is nonpolar, so its solubility in water is low.

The structure of urea (National Center for Biotechnology, n. d.) is polar, so it is easily soluble in water, which is also polar.

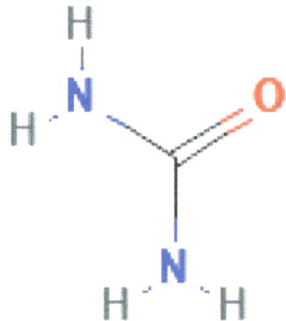

Using the Why Question study method, a flashcard created for this point could be as follows:

Why does urea dissolve in water and uric acid does not?

In birds and reptiles, uric acid is excreted as a dry mass.

Urea and water are both polar, whereas uric acid is nonpolar.

Chapter 10
Begin Learning Physical Chemistry

* * *

Executive Summary (especially for readers who are not chemists):

This chapter illustrates the dynamic nature of planning and executing study methods with the Learning Tool Kit. Notice below, that while making the study plan, a switch from the Decision Tree to the Flowchart was necessary to accommodate more detailed reasoning.

Later, while following the plan, when the time arrived to employ the study methods of Re-reading and Highlighting or Underlining, they had already been utilized and could therefore be skipped. Instead, from the Flowchart, the Summarizing method was identified as the appropriate next step.

Before diving into Summarizing, a continuation of the current step was needed for more Pre-Writing by making observations and writing any strategies that come to mind. During the Summarizing process, a break was taken to employ the Interleaved Practice study method to compare and contrast similar concepts before returning to Summarizing.

Upon reviewing the planned Why Question and Self-explanation study methods, one realizes that only the Why Question method appears to be needed at this time. The anticipated need for the Self-explanation study method may well come into play later when studying new learning objects resulting from applying the Learner-Generated Scenario study method. Thus, the study plan proceeds to apply the remaining study methods straightforwardly.

* * *

Since physical chemistry is generally an overwhelming subject, the Beachhead Strategy is anticipated to be beneficial. In the prologue of the text (Atkins, et al.), the concept of *Boltzmann distribution* is highlighted as a link between molecular energy and the energy of bulk matter and is said to be one of the most valuable concepts in chemistry. Thus, the study commences by defining this concept in lay terms and learning it by planning our study method choices using the Decision Tree.

{(1) Yes, (2) Yes, Pre-Writing and Different Viewpoint, (3) Yes, (4) No, (too large), No, (5) Yes, Beachhead Strategy, (1) Take a break before restarting at the beginning to see whether a new learning object has been chosen.} Since a concept has already been chosen for investigation, we have decided not to start over, but to switch to the Flowchart to continue planning the study.

[Q1 – Yes, Q2 – Yes, S1– Pre-Writing and Different Viewpoint, Q3 – Yes, Q4 – No, Q5 – No, Q6 – Yes, S4 – Beachhead Strategy, Q7 – No, S5 – Re-reading and Highlighting or Underlining, Q8 – No, S7 – Why Question and Self-explanation, Q8 – Yes, S6 – Practice Testing and Delayed Testing, S8 – Learner-Generated Scenario, Take a break.]

Purge numbers and Yes/No decisions to yield a study plan.

* Pre-Writing and Different Viewpoint
* Beachhead Strategy
* Re-reading and Highlighting or Underlining
* Why Question and Self-explanation
* Practice Testing and Delayed Testing
* Learner-Generated Scenario

Pre-Writing:

To employ the Different Viewpoint study method, a web search query is entered: "How does the Boltzmann distribution provide a link between molecular energy and the energy of bulk matter?" We could also try using the index in the back of the text to locate relevant pages on the Boltzmann distribution.

Different Viewpoint, web search:

The first source selected (Boltzmann Distribution – an overview | Science Direct Topics) described it as follows:

This concept is the probability for finding states in a system which has different energies.

From the second source selected (Maxwell-Boltzmann distribution law | chemistry | Britannica):

This concept is a statistical description of the distribution of molecule energies in a gas.

Different Viewpoint, text index search:

    Boltzmann distribution

$$N_i \propto e^{-A\beta}$$

        A = ε_i = energy
        β = 1/kT
        N = population of particles
        k = Boltzmann's constant
        T = absolute temperature

    Boltzmann distribution commonly

$$N_i / N = e^{-A\beta}/q$$

    Partition function

        $q = \Sigma\, e^{-A\beta}$ sum over i

    Molecular partition function

        $q = \Sigma\, e^{-A\beta}$ sum over states i, not over energy levels

    Molecular partition function alternate definition

        If g states have the same energy (levels are g-fold degenerate)

        $q = \Sigma\, g_i e^{-A\beta}$ sum over i energy levels (states with the same energy)

    Spectra and Boltzmann distribution

$$N_u/N_l = e^{-(E_u - E_l)\beta} = e^{-h\nu\beta}$$

        N_u = population of upper energy at equilibrium
        N_l = population of lower energy at equilibrium
        Eu = upper energy
        El = lower energy

Equipartition of energy
> On average, the internal energy of a system is shared equally among the available forms. For each degree of freedom of translational motion, energy equals rotational energy.

Beachhead Strategy:
Choose small, stand-alone concepts as starting points toward gradually conquering the vast subject of physical chemistry.

Re-reading and Highlighting or Underlining:
The items chosen from the Different Viewpoint step are sufficient. After considering the Flowchart, the Summarizing study method can be employed at this point. But first, make more observations and record strategy ideas as a continuation of the Pre-Writing study method.

Pre-Writing:
Our Internet search query on how the Boltzmann distribution provides a link between molecular energy and the energy of bulk matter reveals that it uses probability and energy. The Boltzmann distribution provides a total of microscopic contributions to gain the energy of the entire population of molecules in a bulk system. The usual linking of moles and grams might establish the connection between microscopic and bulk energy.

Summarizing:
<u>Boltzmann distribution</u> can be explained as follows: The population of molecules at a specific energy level is proportional to the base of the natural logarithm raised to the negative power of the product of that level's energy times the reciprocal the product of the Boltzmann's constant and the absolute temperature at thermal equilibrium.

<u>Boltzmann distribution commonly</u> means this: The left side of the Boltzmann distribution divided by the whole molecule population equals the right divided by the partition function.

<u>The partition function</u> and <u>molecular partition function</u> are similar in appearance, so we should use the Interleaved Practice study method to avoid confusing these two concepts with each other. Afterward, return to Summarizing.

Interleaved Practice:

On checking the text information, you may find that the three items are different ways of looking at the same concept, "partition function." Hence, group the following under one heading: partition function, molecular partition function and molecular partition function—alternate definition. Also, remove the word "molecular" from the summary above for Boltzmann distribution commonly. Then, continue Summarizing.

Summarizing (Redo):

<u>Boltzmann distribution commonly</u> means this: The left side of the Boltzmann distribution divided by the whole population of molecules equals the right divided by the partition function.

<u>The partition function</u> is the sum of energy levels that forms the denominator of the Boltzmann distribution commonly.

Summarizing:

<u>Spectra and Boltzmann distribution</u> means this: By using the upper and lower populations and energies at thermal equilibrium, the equation calculates the energy of light absorption or emission.

<u>Equipartition of energy</u> means this: On average, the internal energy of a system is shared equally among the available forms. For each degree of freedom of translational motion, energy equals rotational energy.

Why Question:

Why is the Boltzmann distribution important in chemistry? Answer: The Boltzmann distribution can be used to interpret the following four important concepts: 1) all thermodynamic properties, 2) the dependence of chemical equilibrium constants on temperature, 3) chemical reaction rates, and 4) the occurrence of states of matter.

Practice Testing and Delayed Testing:

Create flashcards to study the learning objects obtained using the Summarizing and Why Question study methods.

Learner-Generated Scenario:

Create an analogy (Simple as Pie study method) to aid in learning the terms related to the partition function.

One analogy could be related to school grades, where numerical grades correspond to states, and letter grades correspond to energy levels.

For example, consider the number of students on a class roster (N) as 25. The numerical grades displayed in the table below show how the students are distributed.

Numerical grades (representing states)

100				
99	89	79 2	69	<60
98	88 1	78 1	68	
97	87	77	67 1	
96 1	86 2	76 2	66	
95	85	75 3	65 1	
94 1	84	74 1	64	
93	83 1	73	63	
92 1	82 3	72 1	62	
91	81	71	61	
90	80 1	70 2	60	
───	───	───	───	───
3	8	12	2	0
A	B	C	D	F

Letter grades (representing energy levels)

Sum over energy levels: q = 3 + 8 + 12 + 2 + 0 = 25

Sum over states: q = 1 + 1 + 1 + 1 + 2 + 1 + 3+ 1 + 2 + 1 + 2 + 3 + 1 + 1 + 2 + 1 + 1 = 25

Notice that the sum over energy levels and the sum over states have the same totals.

To continue the analogy, for example, view the letter grades D or A as representing energy levels, which are two- or three-fold degenerate.

An example is shown on the following flashcard:

> Boltzmann distribution importance
> (What does it help to explain or interpret?)
>
>
> (Use Mental Imagery)

> Imagine four pictures:
>   upper left: a propeller
>   lower left: a "T" followed by an arrow pointing to a "k"
>   lower right: a running shoe
>   upper right: the outline of one of the US states
> These pictures remind of:
>   Thermodynamic PROPERTIES
>   TEMPERATURE dependance of equilibrium constant k
>   SPEED of a chemical reaction
>   occurrence of a STATE of matter

Study Methods Symbol Key

Pre-Writing

Different Viewpoint

Interleaved Practice

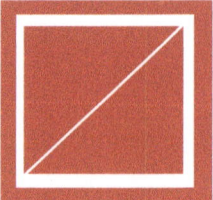
Divide Big Problems

Beachhead Strategy

Summarizing

Re-reading

Highlighting or Underlining

Why Question

Self-explanation

Keyword or Mnemonic

Mental Imagery

Simple as Pie

Practice Testing

Delayed Testing

Learner-Generated Scenario

Chapter 11
Background

This section summarizes the research on the effectiveness of study methods to help you decide which study methods are most effective based on your learning preferences. Dunlosky et al. assessed several study methods as having low effectiveness, partly because more research is needed. Three methods were rated as moderately effective, but missed the high-efficacy designation due to insufficient data.

Relating Better to the Subject

In this section, the author introduces four study methods to complement those reviewed by Dunlosky et al., providing learners with more weapons to combat confusion.

 Pre-Writing

A five-year study in Canada (Kalman et al., 2015) involving approximately a thousand students found that the Pre-Writing study method significantly helped students to learn physics compared to a control group that only wrote summaries of text material.

 Different Viewpoint

The Different Viewpoint study method has proven helpful in teaching students how to switch perspectives (Bollen et al., 2016). Interviews with students studying electrodynamics showed augmented mathematical understanding as they used multiple ways to view a problem. The concepts of divergence and curl of an electromagnetic field were approached in three different ways: graphical representations, mathematical calculations, and the differential form of Maxwell's equations. Mistakes that resulted in contradictory answers when using the different approaches were mitigated by discussing them.

 Interleaved Practice

The Interleaved Practice study method is the only method in Step One that was evaluated by Dunlosky, who rated its efficacy as moderate. Experiments have shown benefits for learners as young as fourth grade, except for low-skilled learners who did not show improvement.

 Divide Big Problems

The Divide Big Problems study strategy was included to assist learners in approaching relatively large learning objects, though it was not evaluated by Dunlosky.

 Beachhead Strategy

The term "beachhead strategy" was borrowed from the Allied troop invasion at the beach in Normandy. This study method, although not evaluated by Dunlosky, helps the learner tackle learning objects that appear overwhelming.

Identifying Learning Objects

This *Manual* presents three study methods to gather the data to be learned. Though Dunlosky et al. evaluated all three methods as having low efficacy, this *Manual* distinguishes them from actual study methods, understanding that methods to merely gather information are not of the same scope as study methods, which explains the low rating. The researchers who explored the Pre-Writing study method used summarizing for their control group (See Background).

 **Summarizing**

Prior training helps in writing good summaries. However, summarizing is difficult for young elementary students and those untrained in the process. Dunlosky's low efficacy rating is partly due to the relatively large amount of time and effort required to train the learner. To use the Summarizing study method effectively, write well by identifying and including essential information while excluding unimportant information.

Most experiments with summarizing have been done at the undergraduate level, where the learning benefits are high. Middle-school students also benefited from it after extensive training on how to write effective summaries.

 Re-reading

Re-reading or hearing a narrative of previously studied material is highly beneficial for learners from third grade to graduate level. Several surveys have shown that roughly 65 percent of college students use the Re-reading method to prepare for tests. Also, the second re-reading is more helpful than subsequent re-readings. Even though Dunlosky rated the Re-reading study method as having low efficacy, this manual has added other proven methods to it, increasing its effectiveness.

 Highlighting or Underlining

Dunlosky rated Highlighting or Underlining as low in effectiveness though this method is popular among learners. However, this manual adds to the technique by complementing it with other methods. The ability to identify the learning objects, rather than mark the text with a highlighter or pen, is the main skill needed to employ this study method.

Making Learning Objects Memorable

Among the five study methods that help prepare data for memorization, Dunlosky et al. evaluated the first four of them. The first two had an efficacy rating of moderate, and the last two were rated as having low efficacy. This *Manual* frequently employs the two low-efficacy study methods in tandem to provide learners with an approach for recalling details from text summaries or charts.

 **Why Question**

Dunlosky ranks the Why Question study method as moderately effective; however, younger elementary students may lack sufficient prior knowledge to properly devise and answer why questions. Theoreticians generally agree that stimulating the integration of new information with extant prior knowledge enhances learning through elaborative interrogation, enabling better recall. Fourth graders through college students have benefited from the Why Question study method. The major reason that Dunlosky withheld a higher rating of efficacy is the lack of research on the generalizability of the effects.

 Self-explanation

Dunlosky ranks the Self-explanation study method as moderately effective. This method allows learners to mentally wrestle with learning objects to explain some aspects. Its applicability extends beyond solving math problems to the use of various facts, concepts or skills. The main key to its effectiveness lies in training learners to explain their thinking while learning, which will lead to gains for learners of all ages.

 Keyword or Mnemonic

The Keyword or Mnemonic study method received a low efficacy rating from Dunlosky, partly due to the limited applicability of this method to appropriate learning objects. Also, the learned information may not be recallable after some time has elapsed. However, experimental evidence strongly suggests that this study method helps enhance learner recall.

This *Manual* promotes the frequent practice of forming memory-enhancing mental images associated with keywords or mnemonics to help recall the learning objects they represent.

 Mental Imagery

The Mental Imagery study method offers a way to study text that is read or heard. Experiments have documented the benefits of this method for third graders and older participants, but the results are inconsistent. Moreover, students younger than third grade did not benefit from it.

In this *Manual*, mental pictures are frequently used also to memorize facts or charts. However, the low efficacy rating by Dunlosky refers to its use during reading or hearing, not with learning objects, such as the facts and charts in this *Manual*.

 **Simple as Pie**

Fred Tidwell, the author's Algebra teacher in ninth grade, taught the Simple as Pie method, which was not evaluated in the Dunlosky paper.

Practicing Recalling Objects

Dunlosky et al. evaluated both study methods in this *Manual* for the forming and use of flashcards. Of the ten study methods evaluated in his exhaustive review, only these two were rated as highly effective.

Due to their high rating, these two methods form the focal point of this *Manual*. The other methods can be integrated with these two methods during study sessions.

 Practice Testing

Dunlosky ranked Practice Testing as highly effective. Although most experiments have been conducted on college students, this method also benefits learners from as young as two years old to older adults and individuals with brain injuries or Alzheimer's. Better readers may experience slightly greater benefits.

 Delayed Testing

Delayed Testing, or "Distributed Practice" in the literature, is a term that Dunlosky uses to encompass several timing aspects of the study. Experiments with more than fourteen thousand participants have shown the benefits of spaced study compared to "massed" study or cramming.

A longer lag time between study and testing can improve recall even in two-year-olds. While most studies have been conducted on undergraduates, this method is also beneficial for people with multiple sclerosis and traumatic brain injuries.

Applying Learning Objects

 **Learner-Generated Scenario**

Dunlosky et al. did not evaluate the Learner-Generated Scenario study method. However, it has been included in this *Manual* to encourage learners to think more about the learning object through practical application.

Epilogue

Concluding with some parting suggestions and information seems beneficial. Beginning with a book or learning source and basic supplies is quick and easy. Gather a few index cards, a pencil and a spiral notebook. Use scratch paper to record your attempts at recalling long or complex flashcard responses. A few examples of flashcards used to study the first few pages of a Math and Physics text (Boas, 1980) are given below. When you have mastered the study methods of this manual, if you desire to memorize larger amounts of material, consider doing a web search for "memory palace" to learn a helpful technique.

Additionally, labeling notebooks on their inside cover and using tabs for flashcards and "recipe boxes" can prove useful. Examples have been given after the flashcards below.

July 3, 2020
A

Repeating decimal → fraction with examples

$a/(1-r)$, where a = repeating portion with decimal point
$r = 10^{-m}$, where m = number of decimal places
$.3333... = .3/(1-10^{-1}) = .3/.9 = 1/3$
$.818181... = .81/(1-10^{-2}) = .81/.99 = 9/11$

July 3, 2020
A

Geometric progression and examples

Sequence of terms, next of which is
prior term times a fixed number
$1, 3, 9, 27, 81 ...$
$1, 4/5, 16/25, 64/125, 256/625 ...$
$a, ar, ar^2, ar^3, ... ar^{n-1}, ...$

July 3, 2020
A

Infinite geometric series and facts

Sum of terms in a geometric sequence
$a + ar + ar^2 + ... + ar^{n-1} + ...$
$S_n = a(1-r^n)/(1-r)$, exists if $|r| < 1$ (convergent)
$S = \lim S_n$ as $n \to$ infinity $S = a/(1-r)$

July 3, 2020
A

Solving story problems with infinite geometric series

Try making an expression that contains an infinite geometric series and then solve it.

July 7, 2020
A

Preliminary Test

To quickly eliminate a series as possibly convergent, check the limit as n → ∞. If the limit is not zero, the series diverges. Otherwise, test further.

July 7, 2020
A

Absolute convergence

To test for convergence for an infinite series which has some negative terms, use absolute values, and a test meant for a series with all positive terms. If this series converges, then so does the original with "-" signs.

Math Physics, convergence of infinite series: (TS-20)

July 7, 2020
A

Comparison Test Part A

July 7, 2020
A

Given a positive infinite series known to converge,
$$p_1, p_2, p_3, p_4, \ldots p_n, \ldots$$
if after some point, like the sixth term,
$$|u_n| \leq p_n$$
then the unknown series also converges.

July 7, 2020
A

Example of Comparison Test A

The positive infinite series of $1/2^n$ is known to converge because it is a geometric series with $r = \frac{1}{2}$, and, $|\frac{1}{2}|$ is < 1. An unknown series of $1/n!$ is considered.
Known = $\frac{1}{2} + \frac{1}{4} + 1/8 + 1/16 + \ldots$
The unknown series $1 + \frac{1}{2} + 1/6 + 1/24 + \ldots$
converges because after 3rd term, the corresponding terms are smaller than the known series.

July 7, 2020
A

Comparison Test Part B

Given a positive infinite series known to diverge,
$$p_1, p_3, p_4, \ldots p_n, \ldots$$
if after some point, like the sixth term,
$$|u_n| \geq p_n$$
then the unknown series also diverges.

July 7, 2020
A

Comparison Test A, with an Analogy

A positive convergent infinite series is similar to a set of black marbles which fit through a hole named Converge. If after some point, each red or black marble of unknown series is same size or smaller, then the unknown marbles also fit (series also converges). (Red means negative.)

July 7, 2020
A

Comparison Test B, with an Analogy

A positive divergent infinite series is similar to a set of black marbles which cannot fit through a hole named Converge. If after some point, each red or black marble of an unknown series is same size or larger, then the unknown marbles also do not fit (series also diverges). (Red means negative.)

In the first paragraph of Chapter 7, you were advised to look for an example of Beachhead Strategy in the Epilogue which demonstrates using the visual paths of the flowchart to pick the best route for choosing study methods. What attracted the author as to a starting point for his Beachhead Strategy for physical chemistry was a statement in the Prologue of Atkins, de Paula and Keeler (Atkins, et al., 2018). It said that the Boltzmann distribution is the link between the energies of molecules and the energy of bulk matter. Also, it stated that the Boltzmann distribution is one of the utmost concepts in chemistry. First, to study this concept, planning with the Decision Tree begins like this: {(1) Yes, (2) Yes, Pre-Writing and Different Viewpoint, (3) Yes, (4) No, (too large), No, (5) Yes - Beachhead Strategy, (1) (Take a break before restarting at the beginning with a new or redefined learning object.)} During the break, proceed with the more detailed Flowchart, which does not assume a new learning object. [Q1 – Yes, Q2 – Yes - Pre-Writing and Different Viewpoint, Q3 – Yes, Q4 – No, Q5 – No, Q6 – Yes, S4 - Beachhead Strategy, Q7 – No, S5 – Re-reading and Highlighting or Underlining…] Notice, by observing the Flowchart, there is another route to get to the Beachhead Strategy. It is [Q1 – Yes, Q2 – No, Q4 – No, Q5 – No, Q6 – Yes, S4 – Beachhead Strategy…]. The former route seems better, because it includes the Pre-Writing and Different Viewpoint study methods.

Note Card Cases

Study Notebooks

References

Atkins, P., de Paula, J., & Keeler, J. (2018). *Atkins' Physical Chemistry* (11th ed.). Oxford University Press.

Boas, M. L. (1980). *Mathematical Methods in the Physical Sciences* (3rd ed.). Wiley India Pvt. Ltd.

Bollen, L., Van Kampen, P., Baily, C., & De Cock, M. (2016) Qualitative investigation into students' use of divergence and curl in electromagnetism. *Physical Review Physics Education Research*, 12. (2) doi: 10.1103/PhysRevPhysEducRes.12.020134.

Dunlosky, J., Rawson, K., March, E., Nathan, M., & Willingham, D. (2013). Improving students' learning with effective learning techniques: Promising directions from cognitive and educational psychology. *Psychological Science in the Public Interest*, 14 (1), 4–58. doi: 10.1177/1529100612453266.

Festinger, L. (1957). *A Theory of Cognitive Dissonance*. Stanford University Press.

Fogiel, M. (Ed.) (1976). *The Physics Problem Solver*. Research and Education Association.

Fortune Palace (n.d.). *Poker Hand Rankings*. Poker hand ranking chart - what beats what?

Garland, T. (2019, Feb. 2). *The Kidney Punch, Liver Shot, and Other Vital Organ Attacks*. www.extremestrikers.com.

Glass jaw. (n.d.). In *Merriam-Webster.com dictionary*. Retrieved from https://www.merriam-webster.com/dictionary/glass%20jaw#:~:text=noun,a%20boxer)%20to%20knockout%20punches

Helmenstine, A. (2017, Jan. 26). *The Periodic Table Wallpaper. Science Notes and Projects*. https://sciencenotes.org/periodic-table-wallpapers/

Hitt, D. (2017, Dec. 19). *What Are Clouds? NASA Knows!* (Grades K-4) Series. *It's a Natural Universe*, (2015, July). www.natural-universe.net.

Kalman, C. S., Sobhanzadeh, M., Thompson, R., Ibrahim, A., & Wong, X. (2015). Combination of interventions can change students' epistemological beliefs. *Physical Review Physics Education Research*, 11,020136.

National Center for Biotechnology Information. (n.d.). *Urea*. National Library of Medicine. https://pubchem.ncbi.nlm.nih.gov/compound/Urea

National Center for Biotechnology Information. (n.d.). *Uric Acid*. National Library of Medicine. https://www.ncbi.nlm.nih.gov/books/NBK273/

National Parks Service, U.S. Department of the Interior. (2018, Feb. 6). *Mohs Hardness Scale*. National Parks Service. *https://www.nps.gov/articles/mohs-hardness-scale.htm*

Nature's Crusaders. (2009, Nov. 28). *The secret life of bird droppings.* WordPress. https://naturescrusaders.wordpress.com/2009/11/25/the-secret-life-of-poop/

Nouchi, R., Taki, Y., Takeuchi, H., Hashizume, H., Nozawa, T., Sekiguchi, A., Nouchi, H., & Kawashima, R. (2012, April 6). Beneficial effects of reading aloud and solving simple arithmetic calculations (learning therapy) on a wide range of cognitive functions in the healthy elderly: Study protocol for a randomized controlled trial. *Trials.* 13(32). doi: 10.1186/1745-6215-13-32.

Panama Canal Authority (n.d.). *Designing the Locks. Canal De Panama.* https://pancanal.com/en/design-of-the-locks/

Petersen, G. & Michael, R. K. (2017). *Physics students' strategies for learning: An investigation.* (Poster). Angelo State University Digital Repository.

Rabbit punch. (n.d.). In *Merriam-Webster.com dictionary*. Retrieved from https://www.merriam-webster.com/dictionary/rabbit%20punch

Sawe, B. E. (2016, August 22). *How Many Countries are in Central America?* WorldAtlas.

Sherlock Quotes. (n.d.). Quotes.net. *https://www.quotes.net/mquote/850562.*

Sucker punch. (n.d.). In *Merriam-Webster.com dictionary.* Retrieved from https://www.merriam-webster.com/dictionary/sucker%20punch

White, J., Van Dusen, B., & Roualdes, E. (2016). The impacts of learning assistants on student learning of physics. 2016 PERC Proceedings, (Jones, Ding, & Traxler, Eds.). *American Association of Physics Teachers.* https://doi.org/10.48550/arXiv.1607.07469

Wilbraham, A. C., Staley, D. D., Matta, M. S., & Waterman, E. L. (2002). *Chemistry.* Prentice Hall.

Young, S. H., (2008, April 24). *Keep a journal to solve tough problems.* ScottHYoung.com https://www.scotthyoung.com/blog/2008/04/24/keep-a-journal-to-solve-tough-problems/

Zimmerman, A. (2016, Feb. 24). Teaching multiplication with the distributive property. Scholastic.

Metacognition and Answers

TS-1 Whizzer

Whizzer: Planning with Decision Tree

{(1) Yes, (2) Yes, Pre-Writing and Different Viewpoint, (3) No, (6) Yes, (7) No, Why Question and Self-explanation, (7) Yes, Practice Testing and Delayed Testing, (8) Learner-Generated Scenario, Take a break}

Purge numbers and Yes/No decisions to yield a study plan:

* Pre-Writing and Different Viewpoint
* Why Question and Self-explanation
* Practice Testing and Delayed Testing
* Learner-Generated Scenario

Whizzer: Actual Learning Attempt with Flowchart

[Q1 - Yes, Q2 - Yes, S1 - Pre-Writing and Different Viewpoint, Q3 - No, Q7 - Yes, Q8 - No, S7 - Why Question and Self-explanation, Q8 - Yes, S6 - Practice Testing and Delayed Testing, S8 - Learner-Generated Scenario, Take a break]

Purge numbers and Yes/No decisions to yield study methods of actual learning attempt:

* Pre-Writing and Different Viewpoint
* Why Question and Self-explanation
* Practice Testing and Delayed Testing
* Learner-Generated Scenario

Note: in this instance the planned study methods and the actual learning attempt were the same.

TS-2 Chess

Chess: Planning with Decision Tree

{(1) Yes, (2) Yes, Pre-Writing and Different Viewpoint, (3) No, (6) Yes, (7) Yes, Practice Testing and Delayed Testing, (8) Learner-Generated Scenario, Take a break}

Purge numbers and Yes/No decisions to yield a study plan:

* Pre-Writing and Different Viewpoint
* Practice Testing and Delayed Testing
* Learner-Generated Scenario

Chess: Actual Learning Attempt with Flowchart

[Q1 - Yes, Q2 - Yes, S1 - Pre-Writing and Different Viewpoint, Q3 - No, Q7 - Yes, Q8 - Yes, S6 - Practice Testing and Delayed Testing, S8 - Learner-Generated Scenario, Take a break]

Purge numbers and Yes/No decisions to yield study methods of actual learning attempt:

* Pre-Writing and Different Viewpoint
* Practice Testing and Delayed Testing
* Learner-Generated Scenario

Note: in this instance the planned study methods and the actual learning attempt were the same.

TS-3 Algebra, circle

Algebra, circle: Planning with Decision Tree

{(1) Yes, (2) No, (4) Yes, Interleaved Practice, (7) No, Keyword or Mnemonic, (7) Yes, Practice Testing and Delayed Testing, (8) Learner-Generated Scenario, Take a break}

Purge numbers and Yes/No decisions to yield a study plan for remembering circle formulas:

* Interleaved Practice
* Keyword or Mnemonic
* Practice Testing and Delayed Testing
* Learner-Generated Scenario

Algebra, circle: Actual Learning Attempt with Flowchart

[Q1 - Yes, Q2 - No, Q4 - Yes, S2 - Interleaved Practice, Q8 - No, S7 - Keyword or Mnemonic, Q8 - Yes, S6 - Practice Testing and Delayed Testing, S8 - Learner-Generated Scenario, Take a break]

Purge numbers and Yes/No decisions to yield study methods for actual learning attempt:

* Interleaved Practice
* Keyword or Mnemonic
* Practice Testing and Delayed Testing
* Learner-Generated Scenario

Note: the planned study methods and the actual learning attempt were the same.

TS-4 Math, multiplication

Math multiplication: Planning with Decision Tree

{(1) Yes, (2) Yes, Pre-Writing and Different Viewpoint, (3) Yes, (4) No, too large, Yes, Divide Big Problems, (6) Yes, (7) No, Self-explanation, (7) Yes, Practice Testing and Delayed Testing, (8) Learner-Generated Scenario, Take a break}

Purge numbers and Yes/No decisions to yield a study plan for remembering what to do when you forget a multiplication fact:

* Pre-Writing and Different Viewpoint
* Divide Big Problems
* Self-explanation
* Practice Testing and Delayed Testing
* Learner-Generated Scenario

Math multiplication: Actual Learning Attempt with Flowchart

[Q1 - Yes, Q2 - Yes, S1 - Pre-Writing and Different Viewpoint, Q3 - Yes, Q4 - No, Q5 - Yes, S3 - Divide Big Problems, Q7 - Yes, Q8 - No, S7 - Self-explanation, Q8 - Yes, S6 - Practice Testing and Delayed Testing, S8 - Learner-Generated Scenario: "12 x 6", Q8 - No, S7 - Self-explanation, Q8 - Yes, S6 - Practice Testing and Delayed Testing, S8 - Learner-Generated Scenario, Take a break]

Purge numbers and Yes/No decisions to yield study methods for actual learning attempt:

* Pre-Writing and Different Viewpoint
* Divide Big Problems
* Self-explanation
* Practice Testing and Delayed Testing
* Learner-Generated Scenario
* Self-explanation
* Practice Testing and Delayed Testing
* Learner-Generated Scenario

Note: planned study methods and the actual learning attempt differ for a new problem, namely 12 x 6.

TS-5 Geology, time scale

Geology, time scale: Planning with Decision Tree

{(1) Yes, (2) Yes, Pre-Writing and Different Viewpoint, (3) Yes, (4) No, (too large), No, (5) Yes, Beachhead Strategy, (6) No, Re-reading, Highlighting or Underlining, (7) No, Keyword or Mnemonic and Mental Imagery, (7) Yes, Practice Testing and Delayed Testing, (8) Learner-Generated Scenario, Take a break} (Repeat for each part.)

Purge numbers and Yes/No decisions to yield a study plan for remembering geology time scale:

* Pre-Writing and Different Viewpoint
* Beachhead Strategy
* Re-reading, Highlighting or Underlining
* Keyword or Mnemonic and Mental Imagery
* Practice Testing and Delayed Testing
* Learner-Generated Scenario

Geology, time scale: Actual Learning Attempt with Flowchart

[Q1 - Yes, Q2 - Yes, S1 - Pre-Writing and Different Viewpoint, Q3 - Yes, Q4 - No, Q5 - No, Q6 - Yes, S4 - Beachhead Strategy, Q7 - No, S5 - Re-reading, Highlighting or Underlining, Q8 - No, S7 - Keyword or Mnemonic and Mental Imagery, Q8 - Yes, S6 - Practice Testing and Delayed Testing, S8 - Learner-Generated Scenario, Take a break] (Repeat for each part.)

Purge numbers and Yes/No decisions to yield study methods for actual learning attempt:

* Pre-Writing and Different Viewpoint
* Beachhead Strategy
* Re-reading, Highlighting or Underlining
* Keyword or Mnemonic and Mental Imagery
* Practice Testing and Delayed Testing
* Learner-Generated Scenario

Note: the planned study methods and the actual learning attempt were the same.

TS-6 Civics, First Amendment

Civics, First Amendment: Planning with Decision Tree

{(1) Yes, (2) Yes, Pre-Writing and Different Viewpoint, (3) Yes, (4) No, too large, No, (5) No, (6) No, Summarizing, Re-reading and Highlighting or Underlining, (7) No, Keyword or Mnemonic and Mental Imagery, (7) Yes, Practice Testing and Delayed Testing, (8) Learner-Generated Scenario, Take a break}

Purge numbers and Yes/No decisions to yield a study plan for remembering the freedoms and rights guaranteed by the First Amendment:

* Pre-Writing and Different Viewpoint
* Summarizing, Re-reading and Highlighting or Underlining
* Keyword or Mnemonics and Mental Imagery
* Practice Testing and Delayed Testing
* Learner-Generated Scenario

Civics, First Amendment: Actual Learning Attempt with Flowchart

[Q1 - Yes, Q2 - Yes, S1 - Pre-Writing and Different Viewpoint, Q3 - Yes, Q4 - No, Q5 - No, Q6 - No, Q7 - No, S5 - Summarizing, Re-reading and Highlighting or Underlining, Q8 - No, S7 - Keyword or Mnemonics and Mental Imagery, Q8 - Yes, S6 - Practice Testing and Delayed Testing, S8 - Learner-Generated Scenario, Take a break]

Purge numbers and Yes/No decisions to yield study methods for actual learning attempt:

* Pre-Writing and Different Viewpoint
* Summarizing, Re-reading and Highlighting or Underlining
* Keyword or Mnemonics and Mental Imagery
* Practice Testing and Delayed Testing
* Learner-Generated Scenario

Note: the planned study methods and the actual learning attempt were the same.

TS-7 Math, inequality

Math, inequality: Planning with Decision Tree

{(1) Yes, (2) Yes, Pre-Writing and Different Viewpoint, (3) No, (6) Yes, (7) No, Why Question and Self-explanation, (7) Yes, Practice Testing and Delayed Testing, (8) Learner-Generated Scenario, Take a break}

Purge numbers and Yes/No decisions to yield a study plan for remembering why multiplying by a negative reverses an inequality:

> * Pre-Writing and Different Viewpoint
> * Why Question and Self-explanation
> * Practice Testing and Delayed Testing
> * Learner-Generated Scenario

Math, inequality: Actual Learning Attempt with Flowchart

[Q1 - Yes, Q2 - Yes, S1 - Pre-Writing and Different Viewpoint, Q3 - No, Q7 - Yes, Q8 - No, S7 - Why Question and Self-explanation, Q8 - Yes, S6 - Practice Testing and Delayed Testing, S8 - Learner-Generated Scenario, Take a break]

Purge numbers and Yes/No decisions to yield study methods for actual learning attempt:

* Pre-Writing and Different Viewpoint
* Why Question and Self-explanation
* Practice Testing and Delayed Testing
* Learner-Generated Scenario

Note: the planned study methods and the actual learning attempt were the same.

TS-8 Math, subtract a fraction

Math, subtract a fraction: Planning with Decision Tree

{(1) Yes, (2) Yes, Pre-Writing and Different Viewpoint, (3) No, (6) Yes, (7) No, Self-Explanation, (7) Yes, Practice Testing and Delayed Testing, (8) Learner-Generated Scenario, Take a break}

Purge numbers and Yes/No decisions to yield a study plan for remembering how to subtract a fraction from a whole number:

* Pre-Writing and Different Viewpoint
* Self-explanation
* Practice Testing and Delayed Testing
* Learner-Generated Scenario

Math, subtract a fraction: Actual Learning Attempt with Flowchart

[Q1 - Yes, Q2 - Yes, S1 - Pre-Writing and Different Viewpoint, Q3 - No, Q7 - Yes, Q8 - No, S7 - Self-explanation, Q8 - Yes, S6 - Practice Testing and Delayed Testing, S8 - Learner-Generated Scenario, Take a break]

Purge numbers and Yes/No decisions to yield study methods for actual learning attempt:

* Pre-Writing and Different Viewpoint
* Self-explanation
* Practice Testing and Delayed Testing
* Learner-Generated Scenario

Note: the planned study methods and the actual learning attempt were the same.

TS-9 Algebra, order of operations

Algebra, order of operations: Planning with Decision Tree

{(1) Yes, (2) Yes, Pre-Writing and Different Viewpoint, (3) No, (6) Yes, (7) No, Keyword or Mnemonic and Mental Imagery, (7) Yes, Practice Testing and Delayed Testing, (8) Learner-Generated Scenario, Take a break}

Purge numbers and Yes/No decisions to yield a study plan for remembering the order of operations in algebra:

       * Pre-Writing and Different Viewpoint
       * Keyword or Mnemonic and Mental Imagery
       * Practice Testing and Delayed Testing
       * Learner-Generated Scenario

Algebra, order of operations: Actual Learning Attempt with Flowchart

[Q1 - Yes, Q2 - Yes, S1 - Pre-Writing and Different Viewpoint, Q3 - No, Q7 - Yes, Q8 - No, S7 - Keyword or Mnemonic and Mental Imagery, Q8 - Yes, S6 - Practice Testing and Delayed Testing, S8 - Learner-Generated Scenario, Take a break]

Purge numbers and Yes/No decisions to yield study methods for actual learning attempt:

* Pre-Writing and Different Viewpoint
* Keyword or Mnemonic and Mental Imagery
* Practice Testing and Delayed Testing
* Learner-Generated Scenario

Note: the planned study methods and the actual learning attempt were the same.

TS-10 Chemistry, diatomic gasses

Chemistry, diatomic gasses: Planning with Decision Tree

{(1) Yes, (2) Yes, Pre-Writing and Different Viewpoint, (3) No, (6) Yes, (7) No, Keyword or Mnemonic, (7) Yes, Practice Testing and Delayed Testing, (8) Learner-Generated Scenario, Take a break}

Purge numbers and Yes/No decisions to yield a study plan for remembering the seven diatomic gasses:

> * Pre-Writing and Different Viewpoint
> * Keyword or Mnemonic
> * Practice Testing and Delayed Testing
> * Learner-Generated Scenario

Chemistry, diatomic gasses: Actual Learning Attempt with Flowchart

[Q1 - Yes, Q2 - Yes, S1 - Prewriting and Different Viewpoint, Q3 - No, Q7 - Yes, Q8 - No, S7 - Keyword or Mnemonic, Q8 - Yes, S6 - Practice Testing and Delayed Testing, S8 - Learner-Generated Scenario, Q8 - No, S7 - Mental Imagery, Q8 - Yes, S6 - Practice Testing and Delayed Testing, S8 - Learner-Generated Scenario, Take a break]

Purge numbers and Yes/No decisions to yield study methods for actual learning attempt:

> * Pre-Writing and Different Viewpoint
> * Keyword or Mnemonic
> * Practice Testing and Delayed Testing
> * Learner-Generated Scenario
> * Mental Imagery
> * Practice Testing and Delayed Testing
> * Learner-Generated Scenario

Note: the planned study methods and the actual learning attempt differed for a second way to remember.

TS-11 Calculus, parts equation

Calculus, parts equation: Planning with Decision Tree

{(1) Yes, (2) Yes, Pre-Writing and Different Viewpoint, (3) No, (6) Yes, (7) No, Keyword or Mnemonic, (7) Yes, Practice Testing and Delayed Testing, (8) Learner-Generated Scenario, Take a break}

Purge numbers and Yes/No decisions to yield a study plan for remembering the equation for integration by parts:

* Pre-Writing and Different Viewpoint
* Keyword or Mnemonic
* Practice Testing and Delayed Testing
* Learner-Generated Scenario

Calculus, Parts equation: Actual Learning Attempt with Flowchart

[Q1 - Yes, Q2 - Yes, S1 - Pre-Writing and Different Viewpoint, Q3 - No, Q7 - Yes, Q8 - No, S7 - Keyword or Mnemonics, Q8 - No, S7 - Keyword or Mnemonics and Mental Imagery, Q8 - Yes, S6 - Practice Testing and Delayed Testing, S8 - Learner-Generated Scenario, Take a break]

Purge numbers and Yes/No decisions to yield study methods for actual learning attempt:

* Pre-Writing and Different Viewpoint
* Keyword or Mnemonic
* Keyword or Mnemonic and Mental Imagery
* Practice Testing and Delayed Testing
* Learner-Generated Scenario

Note: the planned study methods and the actual learning attempt differed for adding another study method.

TS-12 Literature, moral

Literature, moral: Planning with Decision Tree

{(1) No, (6) No, Re-reading, Highlighting or Underlining and Summarizing, (7) No, Mental Imagery, (7) Yes, Practice Testing and Delayed Testing, (8) Learner-Generated Scenario, Take a break}

Purge numbers and Yes/No decisions to yield a study plan for remembering a moral from *Les Misérables*:

> * Re-reading, Highlighting or Underlining and Summarizing
> * Mental Imagery
> * Practice Testing and Delayed Testing
> * Learner-Generated Scenario

Literature, moral: Actual Learning Attempt with Flowchart

[Q1 - No, Q7 - No, S5 - Re-reading, Highlighting or Underlining and Summarizing, Q8 - No, S7 - Mental Imagery, Q8 - Yes, S6 - Practice Testing and Delayed Testing, S8 - Learner-Generated Scenario, Take a break]

Purge numbers and Yes/No decisions to yield study methods for actual learning attempt:

> * Re-reading, Highlighting or Underlining and Summarizing
> * Mental Imagery
> * Practice Testing and Delayed Testing
> * Learner-Generated Scenario

Note: the planned study methods and the actual learning attempt were the same.

TS-13 Chemistry, pouring order

Chemistry, pouring order: Planning with Decision Tree

{(1) Yes, (2) Yes, Pre-Writing and Different Viewpoint, (3) No, (6) Yes, (7) No, Mental Imagery, (7) Yes, Practice Testing and Delayed Testing, (8) Learner-Generated Scenario, Take a break}

Purge numbers and Yes/No decisions to yield a study plan for remembering chemistry safe pouring order:

> * Pre-Writing and Different Viewpoint
> * Mental Imagery
> * Practice Testing and Delayed Testing
> * Learner-Generated Scenario

Chemistry, pouring order: Actual Learning Attempt with Flowchart

[Q1 - Yes, Q2 - Yes, S1 - Pre-Writing and Different Viewpoint, Q3 - No, Q7 - Yes, Q8 - No, S7 - Mental Imagery, Q8 - Yes, S6 - Practice Testing and Delayed Testing, S8 - Learner-Generated Scenario, Q8 - No, S7 - Simple as Pie, Q8 - Yes, S6 - Practice Testing and Delayed Testing, S8 - Learner-Generated Scenario, Take a break]

Purge numbers and Yes/No decisions to yield study methods for actual learning attempt:

> * Pre-Writing and Different Viewpoint
> * Mental Imagery
> * Practice Testing and Delayed Testing
> * Learner-Generated Scenario
> * Simple as Pie
> * Practice Testing and Delayed Testing
> * Learner-Generated Scenario

Note: the planned study methods and the actual learning attempt differed for a second way to remember.

TS-14 Geology, hardness scale

Geology, hardness scale: Planning with Decision Tree

{(1) Yes, (2) Yes, Pre-Writing and Different Viewpoint, (3) No, (6) Yes, (7) No, Keyword or Mnemonic and Mental Imagery, (7) Yes, Practice Testing and Delayed Testing (8) Learner-Generated Scenario, Take a break}

Purge numbers and Yes/No decisions to yield a study plan for remembering order of minerals on Mohs hardness scale:

* Pre-Writing and Different Viewpoint
* Keyword or Mnemonic and Mental Imagery
* Practice Testing and Delayed Testing
* Learner-Generated Scenario

Geology, hardness scale: Actual Learning Attempt with Flowchart

[Q1 - Yes, Q2 - Yes, S1 - Pre-Writing and Different Viewpoint, Q3 - No, Q7 - Yes, Q8 - No, S7 - Keyword or Mnemonic and Mental Imagery, Q8 - Yes, Practice Testing and Delayed Testing, S8 - Learner-Generated Scenario, Q8 - No, Keyword or Mnemonics and Mental Imagery, Q8 - Yes, S6 - Practice Testing and Delayed Testing, S8 - Learner-Generated Scenario, Take a break]

Purge numbers and Yes/No decisions to yield study methods for actual learning attempt:

* Pre-Writing and Different Viewpoint
* Keyword or Mnemonic and Mental Imagery
* Practice Testing and Delayed Testing
* Learner-Generated Scenario
* Keyword or Mnemonics and Mental Imagery
* Practice Testing and Delayed Testing
* Learner-Generated Scenario

Note: the planned study methods and the actual learning attempt differed for a new problem.

TS-15 Poker

Poker: Planning with Decision Tree

{(1) Yes, (2) Yes, Pre-Writing and Different Viewpoint, (3) No, (6) Yes, (7) No, Keyword or Mnemonic and Mental Imagery, (7) Yes, Practice Testing and Delayed Testing, Learner-Generated Scenario, Take a break}

Purge numbers and Yes/No decisions to yield a study plan for remembering which hand beats another in poker:

> * Pre-Writing and Different Viewpoint
> * Keyword or Mnemonic and Mental Imagery
> * Practice Testing and Delayed Testing
> * Learner-Generated Scenario

Poker: Actual Learning Attempt with Flowchart

[Q1 - Yes, Q2 - Yes, S1 - Pre-Writing and Different Viewpoint, Q3 - No, Q7 - Yes, Q8 - No, S7 - Keyword or Mnemonic and Mental Imagery, Q8 - Yes, S6 - Practice Testing and Delayed Testing, S8 - Learner-Generated Scenario, Take a break]

Purge numbers and Yes/No decisions to yield study methods for actual learning attempt:

> * Pre-Writing and Different Viewpoint
> * Keyword or Mnemonic and Mental Imagery
> * Practice Testing and Delayed Testing
> * Learner-Generated Scenario

Note: the planned study methods and the actual learning attempt were the same.

TS-16 Geography, Central America

Geography, Central America: Planning with Decision Tree

{(1) Yes, (2) Yes, Pre-Writing and Different Viewpoint, (3) No, (6) Yes, (7) No, Keyword or Mnemonic and Mental Imagery, (7) Yes, Practice Testing and Delayed Testing, (8) Learner-Generated Scenario, Take a break}

Purge numbers and Yes/No decisions to yield a study plan for remembering how to recite the names the countries of Central America:

* Pre-Writing and Different Viewpoint
* Keyword or Mnemonics and Mental Imagery
* Practice Testing and Delayed Testing
* Learner-Generated Scenario

Geography, Central America: Actual Learning Attempt with Flowchart

[Q1 - Yes, Q2 - Yes, S1 - Pre-Writing and Different Viewpoint, Q3 - No, Q7 - Yes, Q8 - No, S7 - Keyword or Mnemonics and Mental Imagery, Q8 - Yes, S6 - Practice Testing and Delayed Testing, S8 - Learner-Generated Scenario, Take a break]

Purge numbers and Yes/No decisions to yield study methods for actual learning attempt:

* Pre-Writing and Different Viewpoint
* Keyword or Mnemonic and Mental Imagery
* Practice Testing and Delayed Testing
* Learner-Generated Scenario

Note: the planned study methods and the actual learning attempt were the same.

TS-17 Chemistry, simple replacement reaction

Chemistry, simple replacement reaction: Planning with Decision Tree

{(1) Yes, (2) Yes, Pre-Writing and Different Viewpoint, (3) No, (6) Yes, (7) No, Simple as Pie, (7) Yes, Practice Testing and Delayed Testing, (8) Learner-Generated Scenario, Take a break}

Purge numbers and Yes/No decisions to yield a study plan for remembering how to identify a simple replacement reaction:

> * Pre-Writing and Different Viewpoint
> * Simple as Pie
> * Practice Testing and Delayed Testing
> * Learner-Generated Scenario

Chemistry, simple replacement reaction: Actual Learning Attempt with Flowchart

[Q1 - Yes, Q2 - Yes, S1 - Pre-Writing and Different Viewpoint, Q3 - No, Q7 - Yes, Q8 - No, S7 - Simple as Pie, Q8 - No, S7 - Simple as Pie, Q8 - Yes, S6 - Practice Testing and Delayed Testing, S8 - Learner-Generated Scenario, Take a break]

Purge numbers and Yes/No decisions to yield study methods for actual learning attempt:

> * Pre-Writing and Different Viewpoint
> * Simple as Pie and repeat Simple as Pie
> * Practice Testing and Delayed Testing
> * Learner-Generated Scenario

Note: the planned study methods and actual learning attempt differed for redoing analogy.

TS-18 Boxing, rabbit punch

Boxing rabbit punch: Planning with Decision Tree

{(1) Yes, (2) Yes, Pre-Writing and Different Viewpoint, (3) No, (6) Yes, (7) Yes, Practice Testing and Delayed Testing, (8) Learner-Generated Scenario, Take a break}

Purge numbers and Yes/No decisions to yield a study plan for remembering definition of rabbit punch:

> * Different Viewpoint
> * Practice Testing and Delayed Testing
> * Learner-Generated Scenario

Boxing rabbit punch: Actual Learning Attempt with Flowchart

[Q1 - Yes, Q2 - Yes, S1 - Different Viewpoint, Q3 - No, Q7 - Yes, Q8 - Yes, S6 - Practice Testing and Delayed Testing, S8 - Learner-Generated Scenario, Take a break]

Purge numbers and Yes/No decisions to yield study methods for actual learning attempt:

> * Different Viewpoint
> * Practice Testing and Delayed Testing
> * Learner-Generated Scenario

Note: the planned study methods and the actual learning attempt were the same.

TS-19 Chemistry, uric acid

Chemistry, uric acid: Planning with Decision Tree

{(1) Yes, (2) Yes, Pre-Writing and Different Viewpoint, (3) No, (6) Yes, (7) Yes, Practice Testing and Delayed Testing, (8) Learner-Generated Scenario, Take a break}

Purge numbers and Yes/No decisions to yield study plan to remember that bird droppings contain uric acid rather than urea:

* Pre-writing and Different Viewpoint
* Practice Testing and Delayed Testing
* Learner-Generated Scenario

Chemistry, uric acid: Actual Learning Attempt with Flowchart

[Q1 - Yes, Q2 - Yes, Pre-Writing and Different Viewpoint, Q3 - No, Q7 - Yes, Q8 - Yes, S6 - Practice Testing and Delayed Testing, S8 - Learner-Generated Scenario, find structure of uric acid and urea to explore solubility, (new learning object, so start over again), Q1 - Yes, Q2 - Yes, Pre-Writing and Different Viewpoint, Q3 - No, Q7 - Yes, Q8 - No, S7 - Why Question, Q8 - Yes, S6 - Practice Testing and Delayed Testing, S8 - Learner-Generated Scenario, Take a break]

Purge numbers and Yes/No decisions to yield study methods for actual learning attempt:

* Pre-Writing and Different Viewpoint
* Practice Testing and Delayed Testing
* Learner-Generated Scenario
* Pre-Writing and Different Viewpoint
* Why Question
* Practice Testing and Delayed Testing
* Learner-Generated Scenario

Note: the planned study methods and the actual learning attempt differed for a new learning object.

TS-20 Math Physics, convergence of infinite series

Math Physics, convergence of infinite series: Planning with Decision Tree

{(1) Yes, (2) Yes, Pre-Writing and Different Viewpoint, (3) Yes, (4) No, too large, No, (5) No, (6) No, Summarizing, Re-reading, Highlighting or Underlining, (7) No, Self-explanation, (7) Yes, Practice Testing and Delayed Testing, (8) Learner-Generated Scenario, Take a break}

Purge numbers and Yes/No decisions to yield study plan to remember the comparison test for convergence of an infinite series:

* Pre-Writing and Different Viewpoint
* Summarizing, Re-reading and Highlighting or Underlining
* Self-explanation
* Practice Testing and Delayed Testing
* Learner-Generated Scenario

Math Physics, convergence of infinite series: Actual Learning Attempt with Flowchart

[Q1 - Yes, Q2 - Yes, S1 - Pre-Writing and Different Viewpoint, Q3 - Yes, Q4 - No, Q5 - No, Q6 - No, Q7 - No, S5 - Summarizing, Re-reading and Highlighting or Underlining, Q8 - No, S7 - Self-explanation, Q8 - Yes, S6 - Practice Testing and Delayed Testing, S8 - Learner-Generated Scenario, Q8 - No, S7 - Simple as Pie and Self-explanation, Q8 - Yes, S6 - Practice Testing and Delayed Testing, S8 - Learner-Generated Scenario, Take a break]

Purge numbers and Yes/No decisions to yield study methods for actual learning attempt:

* Pre-Writing and Different Viewpoint
* Summarizing, Re-reading and Highlighting or Underlining
* Self-explanation
* Practice Testing and Delayed Testing
* Learner-Generated Scenario
* Simple as Pie and Self-explanation
* Practice Testing and Delayed Testing
* Learner-Generated Scenario

Note: the planned study methods and actual learning attempt differed for redoing analogy.

A Note of Encouragement from the Author

This book challenges us to try new ways of studying. Change can be uncomfortable, and it's easy to make excuses to avoid it. To follow through with the commitment and succeed, we must have a compelling reason for change: improving our results. Some of this book's ideas may seem strange, and you may feel like quitting. However, reading the following slogans from a button in my possession may help. The messages may seem like simple gimmicks, but they recently helped me keep running for another hour after already running for 3 hours and 15 minutes.

+ Don't be afraid to fail.

+ Be afraid of not trying.

+ Stop saying, "We've always done it that way!"

Illustration Credit

Pages 20-22
Decision Tree, Flowchart & Study Methods Chart:
Copyright 2021 by Gary Dean Petersen. *All Rights Reserved.*

Page 40
Periodic Table: Science Notes.

Page 42
Geologic Time Scale:
Natural Universe: licensed under creativecommons.org/licenses/by/4.0/.

Page 45
Epoxy Glue:
Copyright 2021 by Gary Dean Petersen. *All Rights Reserved.*

Page 46
542 Sign:
Copyright 2021 by Gary Dean Petersen. *All Rights Reserved.*

Page 51
Mesozoic & Paleozoic graphics:
Copyright 2021 by Gary Dean Petersen. *All Rights Reserved.*

Page 68
D Integral:
Copyright 2021 by Gary Dean Petersen. *All Rights Reserved.*

Page 71
Test Tube graphics:
Copyright 2021 by Gary Dean Petersen. *All Rights Reserved.*

Page 72
The Mohs Hardness Scale: National Park Service.

Page 79
Map of Central America:
Copyright 2021 by Gary Dean Petersen. *All Rights Reserved.*

All Note Cards & Photos:
Copyright 2021 by Gary Dean Petersen. *All Rights Reserved.*

Christopher and Shary Tompkins, New Mexico, USA – Other illustrations and proofreading
Jeff Miano, Kenya – consultation
Siu Lau, Hong Kong – consultation

The Author

Gary Dean Petersen is a lifetime learner, teacher, world traveler, avid reader, runner and football fan with a strong proficiency in the German language. He holds various teaching certifications, including in Mathematics, Chemistry, Physics, Generalist for Grades 4 to 8, and English as a Second Language. During 2019, he served as an adjunct chemistry lab professor at a Texas university, a STEM tutor at a high school in Kenya and at a Texas junior high school. He holds a Bachelor's degree in computer science and a Master's degree in geology, and he has recently been working toward an advanced degree in physics. He holds several professional memberships, including in the Geological Society of Hong Kong, the West Texas Geological Society and the American Chemical Society. He is currently serving on the board of a Rotary club in West Texas and stays connected with other former staff of Junior Achievement. Mr. Petersen's marriage of more than fifty years has blessed him with children, grandchildren and great-grandchildren.

A Sneak Peek

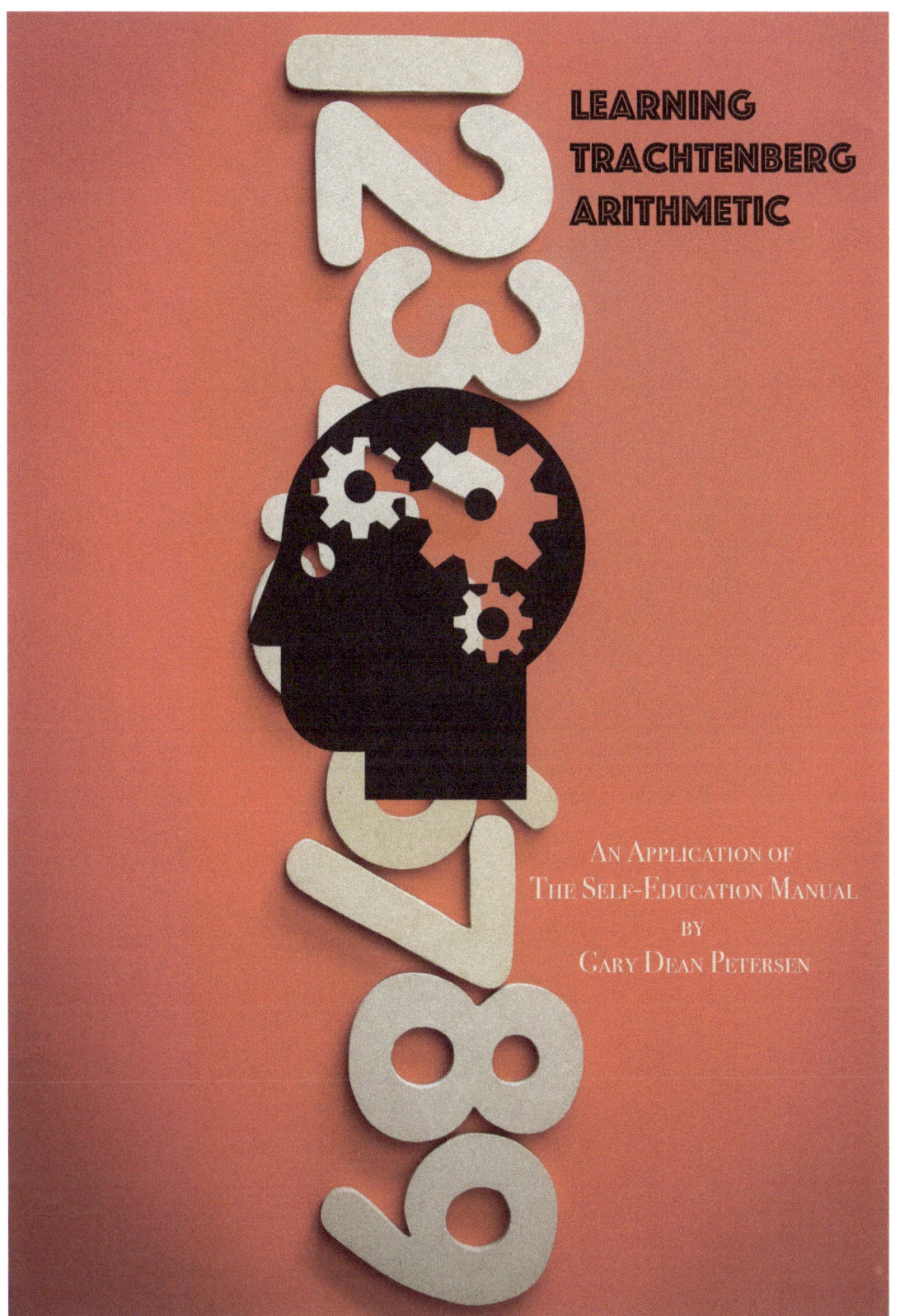

Introduction

During his time as a prisoner of Hitler, Jakow Trachtenberg developed a mathematical system that eliminates the need for multiplication tables and long division. Though the methods may at first seem complicated and pedantic, using the methods from *The Self-Education Manual*, the author of this book attempts to simplify and facilitate easier learning of Trachtenberg arithmetic. First, we will discuss and present the learning material (Different Viewpoint study method), and then, we will apply the SEM study method system to learn the material. The learning objectives will be highlighted in boxes to set them apart from other text items.

Chapter One
General Directions for Multiplication through Twelve

- Write problems horizontally. For example, 592 x 7.

- Append a zero on the left. For example, 0592 x 7.

- Work with digits from right to left, placing each answer digit directly below.

- Sometimes involve the digit on the right.

- Carry as in addition. If none, assume a zero.

To learn these general directions, we will utilize the SEM Learning System, as explained in *The Self-Education Manual*, to create suggested flashcards. Suggested flashcards will aid in remembering the above directions from Chapter One. Looking ahead, as you move on to Chapter Two, you will begin learning how to multiply without relying on the multiplication table up to twelve. For this, we will use the Keyword or Mnemonic and Mental Imagery study methods. For example, we can associate the word "times" with a clock face (to tell time) with the usual twelve numbers arranged in a circle. This clock face will be our "mind palace" for storing memories. Children more accustomed to digital clocks need not worry about using clock hands, as we are not telling the time here.

Below are examples of the front and back of flashcards that you can customize when making your own.

Front of the Flashcard

How should one write multiplication problems to apply these concepts?

Please give an example.

(Use Keyword or Mnemonic.)

Back of the Flashcard

Horizontally.

152 x 7

Keyword is "write."

English writing is done horizontally, from left to right.

Front of the Flashcard

To which end of the problem does one append a zero?

Please give an example.

(Use Self-explanation.)

Back of the Flashcard

To the left end of the problem.

392 x 5 --> 0392 x 5

We can only append a zero to one end of the problem without altering the problem and its answer.

Front of the Flashcard

In what order do we work with the digits of the problem?

(Use Simple as Pie.)

Back of the Flashcard

From right to left, placing the answer directly beneath.

The order is analogous to that of traditional multiplication.

Front of the Flashcard

Which of the two nearby digits might you also involve?

(Use Why Question.)

Back of the Flashcard

The digit on the right.

As we work from right to left, would it make any sense to use a digit not yet reached?

Front of the Flashcard

What if our work should produce more than one digit to write below?

(Use Simple as Pie.)

Back of the Flashcard

Carry when appropriate.

The process is analogous to usual addition problems.

Chapter Two
Multiplication without Tables, Up to Twelve

We will skip the trivially easy problems of multiplying by 0, 1, 2 or 10. To facilitate understanding, visualize the face of an analog clock with the numbers 1, 2 and 10 missing. Please note that for multiplying by 3 and 4, the author provided alternative methods that seem simpler and quicker than Trachtenberg's techniques.

Multiplication by 3: Add Double

Explanation or definition: Add to the current digit its double.

1st example: 13 x 3

Carry (if any)
        013 x 3
Answer: **39**

2nd example: 98503 x 3

Carry (if any) 221
        098503 x 3
Answer: **295509**

Picture a clock face with the number 3 touching a chin, as described on the back side of the flashcard shown below.

Front of the Flashcard

Multiplication by 3

(Use Mental Imagery.)

Back of the Flashcard

Add Double.
Add to the current digit its double.

See a face above, touching the 3 so as to ADD DOUBLE chin.

> **Multiplication by 4: Double Twice**
> Explanation or definition: Double the current digit and then double the answer.

    1st example: 13 x 4   2nd example: 98503 x 4

    Carry (if any) 1   Carry (if any) 332 1
                  013 x 4   098503 x 4
    Answer: **52**   Answer: **394012**

At the position of the 4 on the clock face, visualize four cells of a growing embryo.

Front of the Flashcard

Multiplication by 4

(Use Mental Imagery.)

Back of the Flashcard

Double Twice.
Double the current digit and then double the answer.

See the four cells of a growing embryo.
It had to DOUBLE TWICE.

> **Multiplication by 5: Half and 5**
> Explanation or definition: Take half of the digit on the right omitting decimals, if any, and to that, add 5 if the current digit is odd.

1st example: 13 x 5   2nd example: 98503 x 5

Carry (if any)   Carry (if any)
       013 x 5   098503 x 5
Answer: **65**   Answer: **492515**

To the left of the position of the 5 on a clock face, visualize a half circle.

Front of the Flashcard

Multiplication by 5

(Use Mental Imagery.)

Back of the Flashcard

Half and 5
Take the largest whole number less than or equal to half of the digit to the right, add 5 if the current digit is odd.
The half circle and 5 couple with a whole-number basketball analogy. Take the largest possible number of basketballs, not to exceed half of the zero to nine basketballs from the bin on the right. Then add five more if the left bin holds an odd number.

Multiplication by 6: Add Half and 5

Explanation or definition: To the current digit add Half and 5.

1st example: 13 x 6	1st example: 98503 x 6
Carry (if any)	Carry (if any) 111
013 x 6	098503 x 6
Answer: **78**	Answer: **591018**

Associate "(5)" with "Half and 5." At the position of 6 on the clock, picture "+(5)".

Front of the Flashcard

Multiplication by 6

(Use Keyword or Mnemonic.)

Back of the Flashcard

Add Half and 5

+ (5) reminds of Add Half and 5

Multiplication by 7: Double and Add Half and 5

Explanation or definition: Double the current digit and add Half and 5.

1st example: 13 x 7

Carry (if any) 1
           013 x 7
Answer: **91**

2nd example: 98503 x 7

Carry (if any) 211 1
           098503 x 7
Answer: **689521**

Associate "(2)" with "Double" and "(6)" with "Add Half and 5." At the position of 7 on the clock, picture "(2) and (6)".

Front of the Flashcard

Multiplication by 7

(Use Keyword or Mnemonic.)

Back of the Flashcard

Double and Add Half and 5

Seeing (2) and (6) reminds to double the digit itself, and Add Half and 5.

Multiplication by 8:

a. Start Sub 10 and Double
Explanation or definition: Subtract the current digit from 10 and double the answer only for the rightmost digit.

b. Continue Sub 9 and Double and Add Right
Explanation or definition: For each subsequent digit, subtract the current digit from 9, "double" the answer and "add right" (add to the digit on the right).

c. Finish Left Zero
Explanation or definition: Finish by replacing the leftmost digit's answer with 0.

1st example: 13 x 8   2nd example: 98503 x 8

Carry (if any) 21   Carry (if any)   121
              013 x 8   098503 x 8
Answer: **0104**   Answer: **0788024**

Define Sub 10 to mean: Subtract the current digit from 10. Define Sub 9 to mean: Subtract the current digit from 9. Define (11) to mean Add Right (Add in the digit on the right.). Define (0) to mean "replace the leftmost answer digit with 0." At the position of 8 on the face of the clock, visualize a: Sub 10 and (2), b: Sub 9 and (2) and (11), c: (0).

Multiplication by 9:

a. Start Sub 10
Explanation or definition: Subtract the current digit from 10.

b. Continue Sub 9 and Add Right
Explanation or definition: For each subsequent digit, subtract the current digit from 9 and "Add Right" (Add in the digit on the right).

c. Finish Left Zero
Explanation or definition: Finish by replacing the leftmost digit with 0.

1st examples: 13 x 9   2nd examples: 98503 x 9

Carry (if any) 1   Carry (if any)   1
              013 x 9   098503 x 9
Answer: **0117**   Answer: **0886527**

Multiplication by 11: Add Right

Explanation or definition: To the current digit, add in the digit on the right.

    1st example: 13 x 11   2nd example: 98503 x 11

    Carry (if any)   Carry (if any)   11
            013 x 11   098503 x 11
    Answer: **143**   Answer: **1083533**

Multiplication by 12: Double and Add Right

Explanation or definition: Double the current digit and "add right."

    1st example: 13 x 12   2nd example: 98503 x 12

    Carry (if any)   Carry (if any)   221
            013 x 12   098503 x 12
    Answer: **156**   Answer: **1182036**

Some Suggested Flashcards

Flashcard Front		Flashcard Back
Clue	*Lower Corner Comment*	*Answer*
Clock face showing 1	Use Mental Imagery	Nothing, because it is easy to do
Clock face showing 2	Use Mental Imagery	Nothing, because it is easy to do
Clock face showing 3	Use Mental Imagery	(3)
Clock face showing 4	Use Mental Imagery	(2) (2)
Clock face showing 5	Use Mental Imagery	A half circle followed by a 5
Clock face showing 6	Use Mental Imagery	+ (5)
Clock face showing 7	Use Mental Imagery	(2) and (6)
Clock face showing 8	Use Mental Imagery	a: (10) and (2) b: (9) and (2) and (11) c: (0)
Clock face showing 9	Use Mental Imagery	a: (10) b: (9) and (11) c: (0)
Clock face showing 10	Use Mental Imagery	Nothing, because it is easy to do
Clock face showing 11	Use Mental Imagery	(11)
Clock face showing 12	Use Mental Imagery	(2) and (11)
a:	Use Keyword or Mnemonic	Applies only to the rightmost digit
b:	Use Keyword or Mnemonic	Beyond the rightmost digit (all other digits in turn, right to left)
c: (0)	Use Keyword or Mnemonic	Change the leftmost answer digit to 0
(3)	Use Keyword or Mnemonic	Add to the current digit its double
+ (5)	Use Keyword or Mnemonic	Add Half and 5
(6)	Use Keyword or Mnemonic	+ (5)
(10)	Use Keyword or Mnemonic	Subtract the current digit from 10
(9)	Use Keyword or Mnemonic	Subtract the current digit from 9
(11)	Use Keyword or Mnemonic	Add Right

A Sneak Peek

About the Cover

The cover picture is in memory of Alfred Hess, a high school friend. Al was exceptionally skilled with mechanical tasks on his bicycle and motorcycle. He was his class champion in geometry, and in the final contest, he amazed the judges by finding three ways to prove a problem and selecting the fastest approach. Al did not want to pursue a college education. Instead, he accepted a career as a machinist with an airline manufacturer, where he used his trigonometry skills extensively.

Introduction

There are several compelling reasons for writing **Learning Plane Trigonometry**. Trigonometry is a subject where textbooks recommend self-study to memorize numerous definitions and theorems (Heineman & Tarwater, 1993). The course of plane trigonometry is typically taken in high school or college when students possess sufficient reading and vocabulary skills to understand the earlier general version of the book, **The Self-Education Manual**, where explanations are provided for self-study, which learners can apply to other subjects as well. Also, trigonometry is a prerequisite for several advanced courses in mathematics.

Of course, trigonometry itself has prerequisites, which we will briefly mention to introduce the concepts required for understanding. One such concept is the rectangular (cartesian) coordinate system from plane geometry, which allows us to assign pairs of numbers to designate or plot the location of points on a grid. This grid consists of two perpendicularly directed lines, the x and y axes, which intersect at the origin. Movement in increments or units to the right is in the positive x-direction, and movement upward is in the positive y-direction, marking the boundaries of the first quadrant. Moving counterclockwise around the origin brings us to the second, third and fourth quadrants of the grid. Quadrant two differs from quadrant one as the x values are negative. Similarly, in quadrant three, the y values are negative. In quadrant four, both the x and y values are negative.

Note to the reader:

Personalizing this manual will help you remember the material more effectively. Feel free to check other math references and customize or expand upon the examples herein to suit your background, life experiences and preferences. In this way, the uniqueness of each individual will not hinder the benefits the reader obtains from this material.

Let us begin now.

Chapter One: Preliminary Concepts

One of the first learning objects in this book is the distance formula; however, before that, we will introduce a couple of other ideas. It would be beneficial to review the Pythagorean theorem, and before that, we will discuss the concept of a right triangle using an easy example.

Learning object: 3-4-5 triangle

Any triangle with sides that are 3, 4 and 5 units long forms a right triangle.

The raw Decision Tree choices are shown below (for an explanation of the following paragraph, refer to *The Self-Education Manual*):

{(1) Yes, (2) Yes, Pre-Writing and Different Viewpoint, (3) No, (6) Yes, (7) No, Simple as Pie, and Self-explanation, (7) Yes, Use Practice Testing and Delayed Testing, (8) Learner-Generated Scenario, Take a Break}

During the Pre-Writing and Different Viewpoint study methods, you will discover that this special triangle was used by Egyptians in building pyramids and has also been used by carpenters. You can model this learning object as an exercise for the Learner-Generated Scenario. Try the following exercise:

Place a 3" by 5" index card horizontally on a surface. Center another index card (rotated 90 degrees) on top of the first card and align them along their bottom edges. Take a third index card and position its long edge from the bottom right corner of the first card to the upper left intersection of the first two cards. This exercise shows that a 3–4–5 triangle is a right triangle.

Flashcard clue: Any triangle with sides of 3, 4 and 5 units long...

Flashcard answer: ...is a right triangle.

Learning Plane Trigonometry

Front of the Flashcard

3-4-5 triangle

Any triangle with sides of 3, 4 and 5 units...

(Use Simple as Pie.)

Back of the Flashcard

...is a right triangle.

Place a 3" by 5" index card horizontally on a surface. Center another index card (rotated 90 degrees) on top of the first card and line them up along their bottom edges. Take a third index card and reach its long edge from the bottom right corner of the first card to the upper left intersection of the first two cards. This exercise shows that a 3, 4, 5 triangle is a right triangle.

Learning object: Pythagorean theorem

The Pythagorean theorem states that, in a right triangle, the square of the hypotenuse, c, equals the sum of the squares of the other two sides, a and b. That is, $c^2 = a^2 + b^2$.

The raw Decision Tree choices are shown below (for an explanation of the following paragraph, refer to *The Self-Education Manual*):

{(1) Yes, (2) Yes, Pre-Writing and Different Viewpoint, (3) No, (6) Yes, (7) No, Simple as Pie and Self-explanation, (7) Yes, Practice Testing and Delayed Testing, (8) Learner-Generated Scenario, Take a break}

While practicing the Pre-Writing and Different Viewpoint study methods, imagine demonstrating the Pythagorean theorem by using the 3–4–5 triangle. To wit, let c = 5, a = 3 and b = 4. Then ($c^2 = a^2 + b^2$) becomes (25 = 9 + 16), which is true.

Flashcard clue: The Pythagorean theorem states... Use Simple as Pie.

Flashcard answer: ... that, in a right triangle, the square of the hypotenuse, c, equals the sum of the squares of the other two sides, a and b. That is $c^2 = a^2 + b^2$.

Front of the Flashcard

Pythagorean theorem

The Pythagorean theorem states...

(Use Simple as Pie.)

Back of the Flashcard

...in a right triangle, the square of the hypotenuse c, equals the sum of the squares of the other two sides: a and b. That is, $c^2 = a^2 + b^2$.

Let $c = 5$, $a = 3$ and $b = 4$. Then ($c^2 = a^2 + b^2$) becomes (25 = 9 + 16), which is true.

Learning object: Distance formula

The distance formula states that the distance between two points on a cartesian grid, (x_1, y_1) and (x_2, y_2) is d = $\sqrt{(x_2-x_1)^2 + (y_2-y_1)^2}$.

The raw Decision Tree choices are shown below (for an explanation of the following paragraph, refer to *The Self-Education Manual*).

{(1) Yes, (2) Yes, Pre-Writing and Different Viewpoint, (3) Yes, (4) No, too large, Yes, Divide Big Problems; Notice that, after dividing, each part becomes a new learning object, so we start over with the Decision Tree for each new object.}

While practicing the Pre-Writing and Different Viewpoint study methods, note that the distance formula could be divided into two steps: (1) construction of a right triangle, and (2) calculating the distance using the Pythagorean theorem.

The raw Decision Tree choices are shown below (for an explanation of the following paragraph, refer to *The Self-Education Manual*):

{(1) Yes, (2) Pre-Writing and Different Viewpoint, (3) No, (6) Yes, (7) No, Keyword or Mnemonic, Mental Imagery and Self-explanation, (7) Yes, (8) Learner-Generated Scenario, Take a break}

From the Different Viewpoint study method comes the learning object's name and the basic concept of calculating the distance between two points, (x_1, y_1) and (x_2, y_2). Since x and y are perpendicular to one another, you can construct line segments that are parallel to those axes and touching the two points to form a right triangle. Then, you can use the Pythagorean Theorem to find the hypotenuse, because $c^2 = a^2 + b^2$.

From the Pre-Writing study method comes the inspiration that x and y must have the same units since their squares are being added together in the distance formula. For example, a graph of sales dollars per month would render the distance formula meaningless because dollars and months are different units.

Also, from the Pre-Writing study method comes the insight that if the two points are directly above or below one another or side by side, then either $x_1 = x_2$, or $y_1 = y_2$. In such cases, the subtractions in the distance formula would result in zero. Although the distance triangle can no longer be formed, the result of plugging values into the expressions under the operation of the radical sign still holds true. The reader is encouraged to try a simple example to verify this.

Continuing with Pre-Writing, notice that the middle of the second word has "mu," which is a letter of the Greek alphabet. This can remind us of Pythagoras and his Pythagorean theorem..

When using the Pre-Writing and Different Viewpoint study methods, notice that the first clue word, *distance*, can be transformed by duplicating the first three letters of the word and changing the remaining letters a little (insert "ri" and "l" and then change "c" to "g"), resulting in *distance triangle*.

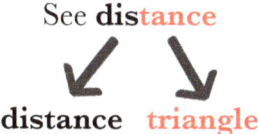

Flashcard clue: Distance formula between two points on a cartesian grid... (x_1, y_1) and (x_2, y_2); use Keyword or Mnemonic.

To calculate the distance between two points on a cartesian grid, draw a right triangle by first connecting the two points (call them $((x_1, y_1)$ and $(x_2, y_2))$. Then, also draw line segments through the points so that each new segment is parallel to one of the axes. Further, apply the Pythagorean theorem to find the length of the hypotenuse, which we will call "d."

Flashcard answer: $d = \sqrt{((x_2 - x_1)^2 + (y_2 - y_1)^2)}$.

For a Learner-Generated Scenario, pick two easy points on a cartesian grid, draw a distance triangle, and calculate the distance between the two points.

Front of the Flashcard

Distance formula between two points...

(Use Keyword or Mnemonic.)

Back of the Flashcard

...d equals $\sqrt{((x_2 - x_1)^2 + (y_2 - y_1)^2)}$.

The keyword "distance" becomes "distance triangle." To calculate the distance between two points on a cartesian grid, draw a right triangle by first connecting the two points, (call them (x_1, y_1) and (x_2, y_2)) and then also draw line segments through the points, so each new segment is parallel to one of the axes, and then apply the Pythagorean theorem.

Learning object: Radius vector

The radius vector refers to the distance r from the origin to a point on the cartesian grid. Its length is positive and can be calculated using the formula $\sqrt{(x^2+y^2)}$.

The raw Decision Tree choices are shown below (For an explanation of the following paragraph, see *The Self-Education Manual*).

{(1) Yes, (2) Pre-Writing and Different Viewpoint, (3) No, (6) Yes, (7) No, Keyword or Mnemonic, Simple as Pie and Self-explanation, (7) Yes, (8) Learner-Generated Scenario, Take a break}

When using the Pre-Writing and Different Viewpoint study methods, notice that the word *radius* reminds us of a circle; in this case the circle is centered at the origin. Continuing this analogy, mentally draw the radius to the point and draw a line segment from the x axis perpendicularly to the point on the circle end of the radius, and another from the origin, along the x axis, to this line segment. We now have a right triangle from which to calculate the length of r using the Pythagorean theorem.

Flashcard clue: Radius vector...

Reminded by the word radius, visualize a circle on a cartesian grid of *radius* r through the point of interest and centered at the origin. Draw a right triangle on the grid and use it to calculate the length of the radius vector using the Pythagorean theorem. The length is always positive.

Flashcard answer: ... r equals the positive $\sqrt{(x^2+y^2)}$.

For a Learner-Generated Scenario, pick an easy point on the grid and calculate the radius vector length associated with the point:
$(0,5) \rightarrow \sqrt{(x^2 + y^2)} = \sqrt{(0^2+5^2)} = \sqrt{(25)} = 5$.

Front of the Flashcard

Radius vector...

(Use Simple as Pie.)

Back of the Flashcard

...r equals the positive $\sqrt{(x^2 + y^2)}$ and is the distance from the origin to a point on the x, y plane.

From the keyword **radius**, see a circle on a cartesian grid of radius r through the point of interest and centered at the origin. Draw a right triangle on the grid and use it to calculate the length of the radius vector, using the Pythagroean theorem. The length is always positive.

Learning object: Standard position of an angle

Standard position of an angle is having its vertex at the origin and its beginning side on the x axis.

The raw Decision Tree choices are shown below. (For an explanation for the following paragraph, see *The Self-Education Manual*).

{(1) Yes, (2) Pre-Writing and Different Viewpoint, (3) No, (6) Yes, (7) No, Keyword or Mnemonic and Self-explanation, (7) Yes, (8) Learner-Generated Scenario, Take a break}

When using the Pre-Writing and Different Viewpoint study methods, try to find a hint in the first word to be used in the clue. Notice that the first word starts with the word "stand." One could think of an angle starting by standing on the x axis. Then let the "x" in "x axis" remind of the word "vertex."

See stand*ard* → standing on the x axis
↳ vertex

Flashcard clue: Standard position of an angle... Use Keyword or Mnemonic.

Flashcard answer: ... standing on the x axis with its vertex at the origin.

For a Learner-Generated Scenario, draw several angles, some in standard position and some not.

Front of the Flashcard

Standard position of an angle...

(Use Keyword or Mnemonic.)

Back of the Flashcard

...standing on the x axis with its vertex at the origin

See <u>stand</u>ard → standing on the x axis
                              ↓
                              → vertex at (0,0)

Chapter Two: Basic Defintions

Learning object: Trigonometric angle

The trigonometric angle is the amount of counterclockwise rotation of the terminal side from the beginning side in the standard position.

The raw Decision Tree choices are shown below (for an explanation of the following paragraph, refer to *The Self-Education Manual*):

{(1) Yes, (2) Pre-Writing and Different Viewpoint, (3) No, (6) Yes, (7) No, Keyword or Mnemonic and Self-explanation, (7) Yes, (8) Learner-Generated Scenario, Take a break}

Notice that the word *trigonometric* could be slightly changed to be read as "try going metric," which reminds us of going counterclockwise to the terminal side with the word *metric* meaning how far the rotation is.

```
Trigonometric → try going    metric
                    |            |
               counterclockwise  how far
```

Flashcard clue: Trigonometric angle... Use Keyword or Mnemonic.

Flashcard answer: ...amount of counterclockwise rotation of the terminal side from the beginning side when in standard position.

For a Learner-Generated Scenario, consider several example angles, some with even more than 360 degrees of rotation or with negative (i.e., clockwise) rotation.

Front of the Flashcard

Trigonometric angle...

(Use Keyword or Mnemonic.)

Back of the Flashcard

...amount of counterclockwise rotation of the terminal side from the beginning side when in standard position.

Trigonometric -> try going   metric
                     | |
               counterclockwise how far

Learning object: Coterminal angle

Coterminal angles are, in standard position, angles having coinciding terminal sides.

The raw Decision Tree choices are shown below (for an explanation of the following paragraph, refer to *The Self-Education Manual*):

{(1) Yes, (2) Pre-Writing and Different Viewpoint, (3) No, (6) Yes, (7) No, Keyword or Mnemonic and Self-explanation, (7) Yes, (8) Learner-Generated Scenario, Take a break}

Visualize the first word of the clue being slightly changed to say "coinciding terminal sides."

Flashcard clue: Coterminal angles... Use Keyword or Mnemonic.

Flashcard answer: ...having coinciding terminal sides when in standard position.

For a Learner-Generated Scenario, one could consider several angles of varying sizes, which also happen to be coterminal.

Front of the Flashcard

Coterminal angles...

(Use Keyword or Mnemonic.)

Back of the Flashcard

...having coinciding terminal sides when in standard position.

See the first word of the clue slightly changed to say "coinciding terminal sides."

Learning object: Domain and range

Domain and range are respectfully the sets of x values and y values of ordered pairs.

The raw Decision Tree choices are shown below (for an explanation of the following paragraph, refer to *The Self-Education Manual*).

{(1) Yes, (2) Pre-Writing and Different Viewpoint, (3) No, (6) Yes, (7) No, Keyword or Mnemonic and Self-explanation, (7) Yes, (8) Learner-Generated Scenario, Take a break}

When applying the Pre-Writing and Different Viewpoint study methods, consider using the name of the clue, *domain*, as a keyword similar to the word *domicile*, marked with x, and the next keyword ranges out from there, but "why?" (sounds similar to y).

Flashcard clue: Domain and range...

Flashcard answer: ...the sets of x values and y values of ordered pairs respectively.

Front of the Flashcard

Domain and range...

(Use Keyword or Mnemonic.)

Back of the Flashcard

...respectfully the sets of x values and y values of ordered pairs.

First word of the clue, **domain**, as a keyword similiar to the word **domicile**, marked with x and the next keyword **ranges** out from there, but "why?" (sounds similar to y).

Learning object: Function

Function means having only one y value for each x value in a set of ordered pairs.

The raw Decision Tree choices are shown below (for an explanation of the following paragraph, refer to *The Self-Education Manual*):

{(1) Yes, (2) Pre-Writing and Different Viewpoint, (3) No, (6) Yes, (7) No, Keyword or Mnemonic and Simple as Pie, (7) Yes, (8) Learner-Generated Scenario, Take a break}

In the Pre-Writing and Different Viewpoint study methods, we could make an analogy. The first word of the clue, function, reminds us of a "functioning" marriage (similar to an ordered pair), in which each x should have only one y (or both partners would become an "ex").

Flashcard clue: Function...

Flashcard answer: ...having only one y value for each x value in a set of ordered pairs.

Front of the Flashcard

Function...

(Use Simple as Pie.)

Back of the Flashcard

...having only one y value for each x value in set of ordered pairs.

The first word of the clue, **function**, reminds one of a "**functioning**" marriage (similiar to ordered pair), in which each x should have only one y (or he becomes an "ex").

Learning object: Definition of the six trigonometric functions of any angle (Too much to learn at once, so we need to reduce it before proceeding.)

Definition of the six trigonometric functions of any angle: steps include 1) placing the angle in standard position; 2) from the origin, moving an arbitrary distance along the x-axis below or above the terminal side; 3) drawing a perpendicular line segment from the x-axis to the end of the terminal side, forming a right triangle of sides: x, y and r; 4) comparing to the following list: sin theta = y/r, cos theta = x/r, tan theta = y/x, csc theta = r/y, sec theta = r/x, cot theta = x/y.

To form the reference triangle for theta, start at the origin, travel horizontally to x, vertically to y and then return on r to the origin.

The raw Decision Tree choices are shown below (for an explanation of the following paragraph, refer to *The Self-Education Manual*):

{(1) Yes, (2) Pre-Writing and Different Viewpoint, (3) Yes, (4) No, too large, Yes, (6) Yes, (7) No, Mental Imagery and Keyword or Mnemonic, (7), Yes, Practice Testing and Delayed Testing, (8) Learner-Generated Scenario, Take a break}

   Divide into several pieces:
   1) Reference triangle
   2) Sin, cos, tan
   3) Csc, sec, cot

Rewrite the learning object into the several pieces. Plan the study methods lists of each of the three pieces by starting over at the beginning of the Decision Tree.

Learning object: Reference triangle

Reference triangle from any angle theta in standard position: starting at the origin, move horizontally on the x-axis a convenient distance, then vertically to the terminal side and return on r to the origin.

For 1) reference triangle, the raw Decision Tree choices are shown below (for an explanation of the following paragraph, refer to *The Self-Education Manual*):

{(1) Yes, (2) Pre-Writing and Different Viewpoint, (3) No, (6) Yes, (7) No, Mental Imagery, (7), Yes, Practice Testing and Delayed Testing, (8) Learner-Generated Scenario, Take a break}

Flashcard clue: Reference triangle...

When you consider the words "reference triangle," let "reference" remind you of a wise owl ready to draw a triangle, and think, "walk, fly, slide over to x, fly to y, slide back to O."

Flashcard answer: ...from any angle theta in standard position, starting at the origin, move horizontally to a convenient x, then vertically to the terminal side and return on r to the origin.

Front of the Flashcard

Reference triangle...

(Use Mental Imagery.)

Back of the Flashcard

...from any angle theta in standard position, starting at the origin, move horizontally on the x axis a convenient distance, then vertically to the terminal side, and return on r to the origin.

In the words "reference triangle," let "reference" bring to mind a wise owl ready to draw a triangle, and think: "walk, fly, slide; over to x, fly to y, slide back to O."

Learning object: Sin, cos and tan

Sin, cos and tan are y/r, x/r and y/x respectively.

For 2) sin, cos and tan, the raw Decision Tree choices are shown below (for an explanation of the following paragraph, refer to *The Self-Education Manual*):

{(1) Yes, (2) Pre-Writing and Different Viewpoint, (3) Yes, (4) Yes, Interleaved Practice, (7) No, Keyword or Mnemonic, Mental Imagery, (7), Yes, Practice Testing and Delayed Testing, (8) Learner-Generated Scenario, Take a break}

When comparing and contrasting sin (pronounced sine), cos (pronounced cosine) and tan (pronounced tangent), notice that the first two have "r" in the denominator, and the third, tan, is the quotient of the other two. Think about how signs, for example, stop signs, stand upright, so sin (which sounds similar to sign) means vertical, hence "y" goes with sin. Think: with "y" out of the way, that leaves "x" to go with cos. To remember that "r" is in the denominator for sin and cos, think of the "y" or "x" as the reference triangle sliding back to the origin while sitting on a radius vector "r." Another way to remember tan is as follows: it is similar to slope, which is "the rise over the run."

Flashcard clue: Sin, cos, and tan… Use Mental Imagery.

Flashcard answer: …y/r, x/r and y/x.

We need to break it up further before learning because it is too much to remember at once.

Learning object: Csc, sec and cot

Csc, sec and cot are r/y, r/x and x/y respectively.

For 3) csc, sec and cot, the raw Decision Tree choices are shown below (for an explanation of the following paragraph, refer to *The Self-Education Manual*):

{(1) Yes, (2) Pre-Writing and Different Viewpoint, (3) Yes, (4) Yes, Interleaved Practice, (7) No, Keyword or Mnemonic, Mental Imagery, (7), Yes, Practice Testing and Delayed Testing, (8) Learner-Generated Scenario, Take a break}

When Pre-Writing and comparing and contrasting, notice that these three items are the inverses of the previous three. Csc (pronounced cosecant) is the inverse of sin (It helps to remember that the first three letters of cosecant are counterintuitive since they remind one of a trig function other than sin). Sec (pronounced secant) is the inverse of cosine. Cot (pronounced cotangent) is the inverse of tangent.

Flashcard clue: Csc, sec and cot...

Flashcard answer: ...r/y, r/x and x/y.

Learning object: Sin and cos range

Both sin and cos range from -1 to +1, inclusive.

The raw Decision Tree choices are shown below (for an explanation of the following paragraph, refer to *The Self-Education Manual*):

{(1) Yes, (2) Yes Pre-Writing and Different Viewpoint, (3) No (6) Yes (7) No, Why Question, Mental Imagery and Self-explanation, (7) Yes, Practice Testing and Delayed Testing, (8) Learner-Generated Scenario, Take a break}

Why must sin and cos be of magnitude less than or equal to plus or minus one? Let the radius vector define a circle centered on the origin and with radius of one. By inspection, no value of x, y or r can be greater than one.

Flashcard clue: Both sin and cos range... Use Why Question and Mental Imagery.

Flashcard answer: ...from −1 to +1, inclusive.

(Why must sin and cos be of magnitude less than or equal to plus or minus one? Let a radius of one define a circle, and inspect possible values of x, y and r.)

Learning object: How do the signs of sin and cos compare to the signs of y and x?

Sin and cos have the same sign as y and x, respectively.

The raw Decision Tree choices are shown below (for an explanation of the following paragraph, refer to *The Self-Education Manual*).

{(1) Yes, (2) Yes, Pre-Writing and Different Viewpoint, (3) No, (6) Yes, (7) No, Why Question and Self-explanation, (7) Yes, Practice Testing and Delayed Testing, (8) Learner-Generated Scenario, Take a break}

When applying the Pre-Writing and Different Viewpoint study methods, notice that "r" is always positive, so it does not determine the sign of a ratio in which it forms the denominator..

Flashcard clue: Sin and cos have the same signs as... Use Why Question.

Why are the signs of sin and cos dependent on the signs of "y" and "x," respectively? Since "r" is always positive, the signs of the trigonometric ratios are each determined by the remaining quantity.

Flashcard answer: ...y and x, respectively.

Learning object: How do the trigonometric functions of coterminal angles compare?

Trigonometric functions of coterminal angles are equal.

The raw Decision Tree choices are shown below (for an explanation of the following paragraph, refer to *The Self-Education Manual*).

{(1) Yes, (2) Yes, Pre-Writing and Different Viewpoint, (3) No, (6) Yes, (7) No, Why Question, (7) Yes, Practice Testing and Delayed Testing, (8) Learner-Generated Scenario, Take a break}

Why are the trigonometric functions of coterminal angles equal? They have identical "x," "y" and "r."

Flashcard clue: Trigonometric functions of coterminal angles... Use Why Question.

Flashcard answer: ...are equal.

Learning object: What do we know about the sum of $\sin^2$ theta and $\cos^2$ theta?

For every angle theta, $\sin^2 \theta$ plus $\cos^2 \theta$ equals one.

The raw Decision Tree choices are shown below (for an explanation of the following paragraph, refer to *The Self-Education Manual*):

{(1) Yes, (2) Yes, Pre-Writing and Different Viewpoint, (3) No, (6) Yes, (7) No, Why Question and Self-explanation, (7) Yes, Practice Testing and Delayed Testing, (7) Yes, Practice Testing and Delayed Testing, (8) Learner-Generated Scenario, Take a break}

Why does $\sin^2 \theta$ plus $\cos^2 \theta$ equal one for every angle theta?

By Pythagoras, $x^2 + y^2 = r^2$.

$\sin^2 \theta + \cos^2 \theta = (y/r)^2 + (x/r)^2 = y^2/r^2 + x^2/r^2 = (y^2 + x^2)/r^2 = r^2/r^2 = 1$

Flashcard clue: For every angle theta, what can be said of $\sin^2 \theta$ plus $\cos^2 \theta$? Use Why Question and Self-explanation.

Flashcard answer: It equals one.

A Sneak Peek

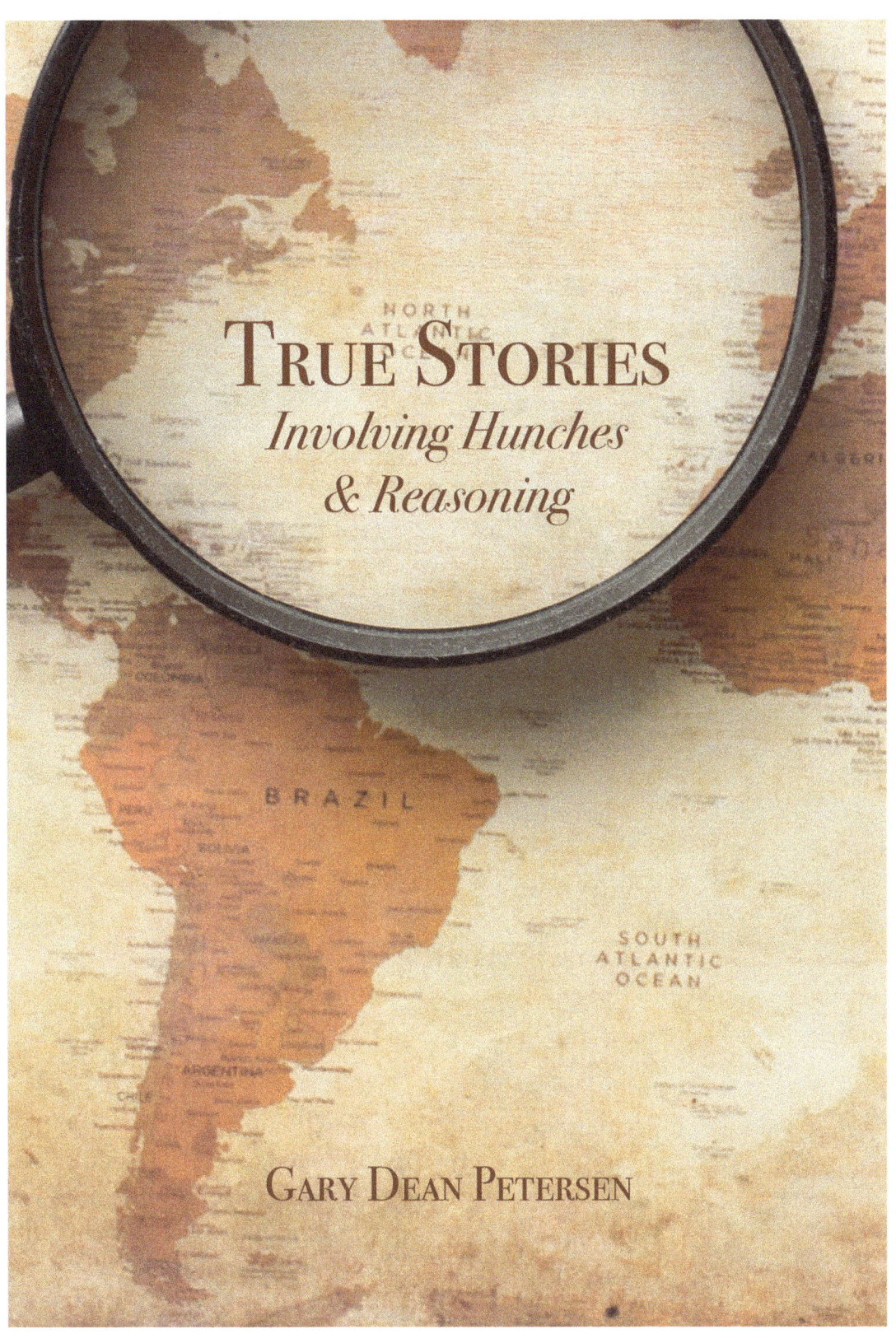

Author's Note

As the author of several self-improvement books, I hope that your reading of this book will yield some beneficial insights applicable to your own life. This book traces the concepts of hunches and reasoning through a few of my life experiences. The memories of these events have seemed somewhat photographic since the moment I became self-aware. Along with my experiences, I have recorded my hunches and thoughts, which I now share with you. In some of these stories, you might conclude that divine intervention may have occurred.

Skunk Saves the Day

Decades ago, during a financial reversal, I did not have enough money to pay my income tax. So, I made a deal with the United States Internal Revenue Service to pay a set portion by the 17th day of each month.

One day, while returning to the car after a college class, I suddenly realized that it was the 17th of May and that I had not yet sent the check to the IRS. At first, I was tempted to just wait until the next day, but a strong urge compelled me to pay the bill immediately.

Since it was already past 7 PM, I knew my only option was the Post Office at the local airport, which accepted mail until 8 PM. So, I hurriedly drove home, prepared the check and the envelope and gathered coins to purchase a stamp from a vending machine.

Soon, I was traveling westward at the speed limit in the dark. My wristwatch showed it was already 10 minutes past 8 PM. Soon, it was 8:15 PM. This does not seem to be working out, I thought. Suddenly, from the north, I spotted a skunk running toward the road. It wasn't apparent whether or not my car had collided with the skunk until I stepped out of the car at the Post Office. The smell of the skunk's spray was very potent.

Undeterred, I entered the Post Office, bought and affixed the stamp and walked to the mail slot on the wall to deposit the envelope. Before doing so, I peeked into the slot to check whether the mail basket had already been emptied. Unfortunately, it had been. Once again, I thought about how things did not seem to be working out.

But then, a woman emerged from the door of the "inner sanctum," where the postal workers were. She seemed to be looking around for something. I held out my envelope and asked, "Can you take this for today's mail?"

Taking it from me, she said, "Sure." Then, glancing around the corners of the room, she said, "You know, I only came out here because we're looking for a skunk."

Storm to the Rescue

Decades ago, when I was a high school chemistry teacher, I began taking evening classes to become a geologist. One day, I arrived at work with around five hours of unfinished homework that needed to be turned in during my first geology course that evening. Since the college classes started almost immediately after a day of teaching chemistry, I realized that the only free time available to attempt the homework would be during my lunch break.

Considering this, I entered the school and taught my first-period class. The second period was not a teaching class but rather a conference or planning period. Anticipating the possibility of rain, right before the second period, I retrieved my college homework from my car. I reasoned that if waited until lunchtime, I might have to get the homework in the rain.

As I reentered the school, I stepped into the faculty lounge just in time to hear an announcement over the public address system: "The weather is going to be too dangerous for students to go outside to change classes, so everyone is to remain where they are until further notice."

Thus, I found myself with five hours of free time to work on my homework, which I finished and later received a perfect grade on. It was an unusual day at the high school, and almost nobody knew that it seemed to be my fault.

Near Death

Once, during my time at a geological field camp as a student, I had a harrowing experience that made me think I may never see another sunrise. The story began the previous evening. At nearly dusk, the professors and students had arrived at the Grand Teton National Park in Wyoming from Montana in three white vans. We were instructed to pitch our tents and deposit any food into the anti-bear bins. These two bins were roughly six to eight feet long and not locked but latched in a manner deemed impossible for a bear to open.

Since mosquitos were ubiquitous, I quickly zipped myself into my single-person tent. After munching on a nutrition bar and drinking water, I relaxed for a bit. When I finally unzipped my tent, the camp was deserted—the vans were missing and everyone was gone! To hunt them down, I picked a direction and counted my steps to ensure I could find my way back. After 1500 steps, I retreated to the camp.

The next morning, I was told that the rest of the cadre had gone out for supper and to shop for groceries for the next day's breakfast and lunch. Four activities were offered for the day, and I had chosen to make a 15-mile hike. Being two or three times older than the other students, I soon fell far behind and could not see the others. I had to hope that the footprints in the snow that I was following belonged to my group. The effort to follow became more difficult as I clambered over a jumble of boulders to cross a fourteen-inch-deep stream of rushing water. After a while, my water supply ran out, so I resorted to stuffing snow into a bottle. I soon found out that it takes a lot of snow to make a small amount of water.

At the halfway point, I finally caught up with my group mates, who were just finishing their lunch break. With only breakfast bars to eat, and not many of those, I soon ran out of food. Again, while following their footprints, I slowed down and stopped to call my wife in Texas to describe my ordeal. She commented that I sounded tired. When I finally reached the van that had brought my group, I felt hungry and weak. The others were waiting on another fellow who had taken a wrong turn. I remember wondering if the weeds and grass near a log by the van were sanitary and edible. The next thing I knew, I was on the grass, twitching and unable to lift my head.

Soon, the professor with our group, who was an ultra-runner, diagnosed me as having, as runners say, "hit the wall." He had some cran-raspberry juice to replenish my sugar levels, as my body had run out, similar to what can happen to diabetics. He explained that the next step would have been unconsciousness, followed by death. He drove us to the headquarters building for the Grand Teton National Park, where I ordered a burger and gradually recovered.

By phone, I informed my wife about the day's events, and she shared the news with our three grown children. Later, she informed me that our oldest child had burst into tears upon hearing the news. Not wanting my daughter to feel bad, I called her. To my surprise, she told me that for the whole day, she had sensed that I was in danger and that she needed to pray for me. No wonder tears overcame her when she realized that her premonition had been correct.

www.ingramcontent.com/pod-product-compliance
Lightning Source LLC
Chambersburg PA
CBHW042357070526
44585CB00029B/2973